ON THE ART OF MEDIEVAL
Arabic Literature

Princeton Essays in Literature

Advisory Committee: Joseph Bauke, Robert Fagles,

Claudio Guillén, Robert Maguire

(For a list of the other titles in this series,
see page following index.)

ON THE ART OF MEDIEVAL
Arabic Literature

Andras Hamori

PRINCETON UNIVERSITY PRESS

PRINCETON, NEW JERSEY

Publication of this book has been aided by the
Andrew W. Mellon Foundation and the
Department of Near Eastern Studies of Princeton University

Library of Congress Cataloging in
Publication information will be found on the
last printed page of this book.

PRINTED IN THE UNITED STATES OF AMERICA
BY PRINCETON UNIVERSITY PRESS
PRINCETON, NEW JERSEY

Second printing, 1975

To my mother and father

Preface

THIS book was written for the student of literature as well as for the specialist in Arabic. Its main concern is with the three aspects of medieval Arabic literature that appear most alien to modern Western taste: the limitation of themes, the sedimentation with conventions, and the use of reticent patterns of composition.

There are three parts and three approaches. The first part (Chapters I-III) is historical: it takes for its theme the transformations in poetic genres and poetic attitudes (towards time and society) in the period beginning with the sixth century A.D. and ending with the tenth. The second part (IV-V) concentrates on some problems of poetic technique: how poems were made to hang together, how conventions were handled. The third part (VI-VII) deals with methods of composition in prose, examining the orders and disorders in two tales from the *Arabian Nights*.

To help the non-specialist, there is a chronological table in the back.

The analysis of literary works resembles linguistic analysis in one respect that some people find unpleasant: a single problem can often be solved in a number of ways, and some rival solutions cannot be ranked until all solutions to all problems are in—in other words, never. The elimination of flaws that render a piece of criticism trivial or invalid—provincial psychology, anachronistic sociology—does not spell the end of multiple explanations. But such is the relation of criticism to the meaning of the work,[1] and certainly criticism is the more enjoyable for its partial character.

[1] Let me quote, as something of a motto, a passage of M. Dufrenne's, *Esthétique et philosophie* (Paris, 1967), 141: "Il n'y a pas une vérité de Racine, telle qu'à l'explorer le critique soit assujetti à la loi du tout

Parts of this book have been published in the form of journal articles. Chapter VI is based on an essay in *BSOAS*, XXXIV (1971); an essay in *Studia Islamica*, XXX (1969) is utilized in Chapter IV and in the last few pages of Chapter II; the middle section of Chapter V is a new treatment of a subject I wrote about in *JSS*, XII (1967). I am grateful to the editors of these journals for permission to include in the book versions of work that they first printed.

I would like to thank Princeton University, the Princeton University Council on Regional Studies, and the Department and Program in Near Eastern Studies for their financial support. I am also obliged to Princeton University and to the Department of Near Eastern Studies for having generously granted the leaves during which much of this book was written.

I wish that my own powers had been sufficient to keep me clear of the many quicksands of sense and style from which my friends and wife had to pull me. For such rescue operations—always time-consuming, often tedious, and at times conducted for the benefit of one flailing at his rescuers—as well as for many helpful suggestions, I am grateful to Lewis Fleischner, Roy Mottahedeh, and Paul Oppenheimer, and most of all to Ruth Hamori. Without her surveillance of this work, I would have fared no better than Edmund Waller's poor son Benjamin, who (as Samuel Johnson relates) was disinherited and sent to New Jersey, as wanting common understanding.

A.H., *November 1972, Princeton, N.J.*

---

ou rien; mais Racine est principe de vérité, il rend vrais les *Sur Racine* les plus divers. Mais n'y en a-t-il point qu'il rende faux? Oui, tous ceux qui ne sont pas vraiment sur Racine, qui ne procèdent point d'une lecture véritable; et peut-être apparaît-il du même coup que la diversité des autres est plus apparente que réelle, parce que c'est vers un même noyau inentamable de sens que convergent, sans jamais l'investir définitivement, tous les itinéraires."

Contents

Note on Translation and Transliteration

UNLESS otherwise indicated, the translations are my own.

The non-specialist can form an approximate idea of the transliterated sounds by consulting the following paragraph.

The vowels of Arabic are approximately as in *pat*, *pit*, and *put*. Each vowel can be long or short. Dots under consonants (which indicate pharyngealized pronunciation) may be disregarded. *j* has its English sound; ʿ is a pharyngeal fricative, and ʾ is a glottal stop. ʾ is heard in German *ge-antwortet, beobachten*, etc. No European language has ʿ, but since historically many Semitic languages have reduced this sound to ʾ, the reader can afford to do likewise. *q* is a [k] sound made far back. *kh*, *th*, and *dh* stand for one sound each: counterparts are *ch* in Scottish *loch*, *th* in *thin*, and *th* in *wither*.

Where assimilation of the definite article occurs, I transcribe the resulting sound. I do not use an apostrophe to mark the *hamzat al-waṣl* in *bābu l-bayti*, and the like: it is cumbersome, confusing, and historically indefensible.[1] When particles of one consonant precede morphs that are never found after juncture, I use no hyphen: *bil-*, *bihā*, etc.; elsewhere I use one: *bi-abī*, etc.

Orthography rather than sound is represented in two cases where the contrary practice confuses me, and I suppose others too. When a final long vowel is followed by a consonant cluster, the vowel is shortened, but this sandhi remains unmarked in the Arabic orthography as well as in my transliteration. In turn, at the end of a line of verse, all vowels are sounded long, but I marked this only when it is signaled by

[1] Cf. T. O. Lambdin, "The Junctural Origin of the West Semitic Definite Article," *Near Eastern Studies in Honor of W. F. Albright*, ed. H. Goedicke (Baltimore and London, 1971), 315-33.

the orthography in the original. Anceps vowels I marked as the prosody required.

Classical prose is transliterated with case endings, modern without.

In transliterating Hebrew passages, I did not mark the spirantization of the letters *b-g-d-ḳ-p-t*. The distribution of spirantized and unspirantized forms is nearly complementary, and such ambiguities as might occur are made up for by the corresponding diminution of typographic clutter. The transliteration of Hebrew vowels is fairly true to the orthography, but a few distinctions (segol/hatef segol, for example) remain unmarked. In transliterating poetry, I did not transcribe final *-h* used as a *mater lectionis.*

With no better justification than that of convenience, in speech we usually deprive Arab authors of the articles prefixed to their *nisba* names. I follow this practice whenever the *nisba* alone appears, since to the non-Arabist the articles are so many exotic adjuncts. On the other hand, many American Arabists might say *Mubarrad* but none *Khansā'*; consequently, I kept articles before other than *nisba* names. To make names less formidable looking, certain construct chains are transliterated as single units: *'Abdalqāhir*, *Sayfaddawla*, etc.

Genres

AND THE TRANSFORMATION OF GENRES

one

The Pre-Islamic Qaṣīda: The Poet as Hero

1

ARABIC literature begins with the poetry of the century or so before the coming of Islam. The voice belongs to nomads of the desert, but it is neither halting nor unsophisticated. What tradition ascribes to the oldest recorded poets is no primitive song, but verse in complex meters, with a polished rhetoric and a precise, carefully managed vocabulary.[1] The development that led to this fluency and mastery of craft is obscure: the span of the pre-Islamic poetry handed down to us is too brief. None of the texts we now have are likely to antedate the early five hundreds. In the pre-Islamic age, poems were orally transmitted and much previous material must have been lost or absorbed into the work of later poets.

In themes and imagery there are scattered links with the older traditions of the Near East,[2] but the earliest Arabic poetry has a flavor that is distinctly its own. In form, the use of rhyme and strict meter is radically new. Neither technique is regularly employed in the other Near Eastern traditions, such as the Egyptian, Babylonian, or Hebrew. A single rhyme

[1] Cf. R. Jacobi, *Studien zur Poetik der altarabischen Qaṣide* (Wiesbaden, 1971), Chapter III, especially the section *Der rhetorische Stil.*

[2] Cf. G. Jacob, *Studien in arabischen Dichtern*, IV (Berlin, 1897) and two articles by C. Lyall, "The Pictorial Aspects of Ancient Arabian Poetry," *JRAS*, XLIV (1912), 133-52 and "The Relation of the Old Arabian Poetry to the Hebrew Literature of the Old Testament," *JRAS*, XLVI (1914), 253-66.

runs through the entire poem, whether it has five lines or eighty; the structure of Arabic word formation is such that this can be achieved without poetic acrobatics. The meters are quantitative, being based on various sequences of long and short syllables, as in Latin or Greek.

In the Arabian peninsula, urbanized commercial centers existed, and at its edge Arab vassals of the Sassanids held court at Ḥīra near the Euphrates. Nonetheless, the desert was the true stage for poetry in the pre-Islamic period, and the life of the beduin tribe supplied the subject matter. A poet was the pride and ornament of his people, for he alone would perpetuate the fame of their noble deeds, dignify the memory of their dead, and trap their enemies in songs of mockery. These functions of poetry determine the major genres. Professional transmitters had the job of memorizing and disseminating great quantities of verse. In some cases at least, the transmitter seems to have been a kind of apprentice to the poet, learning the craft of verse-making in a master's workshop, and later becoming a poet in his own right. It is difficult to say how much the original poem may have changed at the transmitter's hands. Some degree of touching up was no doubt considered acceptable.[3]

A few modern scholars have thought that practically all allegedly pre-Islamic verse is the result of skillful forgery by medieval philologists. In view of the distinctly oral character of the ancient poetry, the accusation is untenable, but it is not easy to tell which of the compositions attributed to early authors are in fact genuine.[4]

[3] We find out in al-Jāḥiẓ, *Kitāb al-ḥayawān* (Cairo, 1966), I, 41, that the poet Dhū r-Rumma preferred written versions of his work, being wary of the changes that must occur in oral transmission.

[4] Formulaic diction as the typical technique of oral tradition is discussed in J. D. Hyde, "A Study of the Poetry of Maymūn ibn Qays al-A'shā" (unpublished Princeton University dissertation, 1970), 95-

There were numerous motives for forgery. The resettlement of the conquering Muslim tribesmen in Syria and Irak brought about tribal realignments and sparked constant political struggles among factions, in which poetry, especially in the twin forms of panegyric and satire, was a weapon. For greater impact, contemporary propaganda must frequently have been cast in the mold of a judgment handed down by the ancients. Some pieces of difficult verse may simply be the work of philologists who had despaired of authentic citations to clarify an odd, rare word, but who were nevertheless resolved never to say die. The collector's pride too must not be underestimated. It indicates the state of affairs that a great collector of ancient verse, al-Mufaḍḍal (died ca. 790), complained that after Ḥammād, a colleague of prodigious memory and obviously great if unscrupulous talents, no one could any longer distinguish old pieces from freshly forged ones. Obvious anachronisms give away verses here and there, but other criteria for establishing authenticity seem arbitrary. It is tempting to accept compositions whose contents accord well with what we know of the poet's environment, and to reject poems that appear chiefly a lexicographer's delight. But we can never be quite sure.

In any event, whatever forgeries the eighth-century collectors managed to foist upon their public, it is quite impossible that they produced a body of verse that is significantly different from the poetry of their own period, without having a considerable amount of authentic material available to them.[5]

---

124. See also J. T. Monroe, "Oral Composition in Pre-Islamic Poetry," *Journal of Arabic Literature*, III (1972), 1-53.

[5] Compare the opinion of R. Blachère, who, if anything, is hypercritical on the point of authenticity (*Histoire de la littérature arabe*, I [Paris, 1952], 186): "Rapprochés des oeuvres composées en la seconde moitié du Ier/VIIe siècle, comme celles de JARĪR ou d'AL-FARAZDAQ,

Consequently, an inquiry directed at the relations among conventions in the old poetry, at the principal stylistic features, and at the transformations of the driving spirit of Arabic verse after Islam cannot be much endangered by the cunning pranks of medieval scholars. Besides, some of the great collections were thought quite trustworthy in the Middle Ages, and there is little reason to doubt their basic authenticity now. Chief among these is al-Mufaḍḍal's anthology, the *Mufaḍḍalīyāt.* A recent study of the collection known as the *Mu'allaqāt* has improved its claim to legitimate descent.[6] In this chapter, I will rely mainly on these sources.

2

Pre-Islamic poetry in Arabic can be reasonably divided into two groups: poems that focus on a single subject; and others that join together a number of ostensibly disparate, loosely connected motifs. The complex poem—the *qaṣīda*—is usually more mannered, descriptive, and predictable than the simple composition. The simple poem often alludes to or narrates specific events; the *qaṣīda*, with which I shall be dealing, tends to employ a sequence of set pieces picked from a rather small inventory of themes. The variability of motifs will be found very low even when compared with such a set-piece genre as the pastoral. Size has much to do with this uniformity: few *qaṣīdas* run over a hundred lines. The success enjoyed by such a predictable genre is intriguing. In the West,

---

les pastiches nous paraissent de fidèles produits de la tradition poétique avant l'Islam. Qu'ils accentuent certaines tendances, qu'ils marquent une prédilection pour quelque thèmes et quelque clichés, nous n'en doutons pas. Mais dans l'ensemble, ils ne faussent ni l'allure de leurs modèles, ni les sentiments que célèbrent les vieux poètes."

[6] M. J. Kister, "The Seven Odes," *RSO*, XLIV (1969), 27-36.

a good deal of modern poetry has embraced the shock value of unpredictability with such ardor that a large segment of our audience now simply confuses unpredictability and ardor; all the more reason then to try to understand the vitality, in other times and places, of unusually conventional genres.

It is impossible to draw up a blueprint of themes and sequences that will account for all *qaṣīdas*. They are poems that make constant use of a common stock; nonetheless, they are works of individual poets. But an outline may be pieced together—fairly rigid for the first half of the *qaṣīda*, more flexible for the second—that can be observed in most texts.

The composite poem, unless it is a work of commemoration, begins with an elegiac section in which a broken-off love affair is recalled. The lady may just be departing with her tribe, the women's camel-litters still visible on the horizon, or else she may have left the poet years ago. In the latter case, the *qaṣīda* is likely to open with the recognition of a place in the desert, where vestiges of human habitation remain despite a return to wilderness and desolation. It is the site of an encampment where the lady's tribe once lived near the poet's.

These scenes are sentimental but not factitious. During the dry season, the tribes had to stay at their permanent sources of water, but when, after the autumnal equinox, the rains had assured ample pasturage and an adequate water supply, they could freely roam the desert with their camels. Thus, during winter and spring, people from different tribes might meet, only to separate as summer and drought returned.

The poet conjures up pleasurable or melancholy moments of the past love affair. The lady's beauty is often set forth in a detailed catalogue. At last the poet decides to stop brooding; he mounts his camel and rides away. The camel too is often methodically described, and there are cases where there is no transition at all between the departure or campsite scene and the camel section.

The second part of the *qaṣīda* gets to the point: the virtues and memorable exploits of the poet, his tribe, or his patron are vaunted; or else a base lineage and contemptible deeds are thrown in the face of an antagonist. The life depicted in sections that celebrate noble qualities is in some ways reminiscent of what Gibbon tells us, via Tacitus, of the Germanic tribes in antiquity: valor in battle and lavish generosity are coupled with prowess at drinking and readiness to gamble. Backdrops vary, but there is a unifying mood. Whether the scene is of war or of a pleasant indolence, in the wings death is crouching.

Beliefs in an afterlife have frequently brought more anguish than joy, and the absence of religious prescriptions does not unavoidably lead to glum preoccupation with a haphazard and meaningless death. But mortality is the nourishment of art, and facing death head-on the first task of the *qaṣīda*.

This task emerges perhaps most clearly from the fact that in the old poetry heroic recklessness often gets the better of the reasoned social norm. In beduin society, bloodshed is usually followed by an arbitrated payment of compensation.[7] Therefore, it is important to notice that pre-Islamic poetry was interested in cases where arbitration failed or was rejected out of hand, and that, aside from the pool of conventional themes, its favorite subject matter was supplied by feuds in which some crooked spirit had turned kin or allies into mortal enemies. Such enmity marked the wars of al-Ḥuraqa, of Dāḥis, of Basūs.[8] As one poet says (*Mufaḍḍalīyāt*, 12:6 al-Ḥuṣayn ibn al-Ḥumām):

[7] Cf. A. Musil, *The Manners and Customs of the Rwala Bedouins* (New York, 1928), Ch. xx.

[8] For the histories of these wars, see Lyall, *Mufaḍḍalīyāt*, II (Oxford, 1918), 288-90 (of Dāḥis) and 33-35 (of al-Ḥuraqa), and Lyall, *Translations of Ancient Arabian Poetry* (New York, 1930) (of Basūs).

yufalliqna hāman min rijālin a'izzatin
'alaynā wa-hum kānū a'aqqa wa-aẓlamā

Our swords split the heads of men who were once very dear to us, but who acted perversely and unjustly.

At bottom, the crooked spirit is an aspect of heroic character: it is the hero's need to play his match with death, never to miss a move in which he can expose himself to danger.

From the very earliest poems on, we often meet the figure of an anonymous blamer who reproves the poet-protagonist for reckless behavior. In reply the poet speaks of the inescapability of death, of the *manāyā* who find one when the hour is ripe. Such is Ṭarafa's answer (*mu'allaqa*, 44):

alā ayyuhādhā l-lā'imī aḥḍuru l-waghā
wa-an ashhada l-ladhdhāti hal anta mukhlidī

O you who reproach me because I am found in the midst of war as well as of pleasure, can you make me endure forever?

There are poems in which war is so much a mere medium for tempting death that we are left in the dark as to causes, factions, and fortunes. In such works in the heroic mode, the antagonist is drawn noble and intrepid ('Antara, *mu'allaqa*, 51):

fa-shakaktu bir-rumḥi l-aṣammi thiyābahū
laysa l-karīmu 'alā l-qanā bi-muḥarrami

I pierced his armor with the solid spear; no sanction keeps the spear away from the noble.

In line 53, 'Antara describes the dispatched enemy as *ḥāmi l-ḥaqīqati mu'limi*, one who protects what he ought to protect, and who displays upon himself a mark to signal that he is a bold champion, eager to be challenged. *Ḥāmi l-ḥaqīqati* is a cliché, and its connotation is more important than its precise meaning, because it is a cliché proper to the heroic dirge, *marthiya.*[9]

To tempt death is the hero's destiny. The crucial thing for the heroic spirit is not so much to go down fighting, as to have a tincture of will in one's death, to see it through and be its master. But a poetry in which poet and hero are a single person will have to deal with a dramaturgical problem: the same person cannot experience death and then talk about it. To put it in another way: having seen something through to the end implies, emotionally if not logically, that you can reflect upon it; and to a poetic statement of mastery over one's actions such afterthought is most important of all. Posthumous fame means that the survivors do the reflecting instead of the hero, but this is solving the problem by sleight of hand. Anticipation of death or burial works by a similar trick, and it can be very effective (*Mufaḍḍalīyāt,* 9:31-33, Mutammim ibn Nuwayra):

yā lahfa min 'arfā'a dhāti falīlatin
jā'at ilayya 'alā thalāthin takhma'u
ẓallat turāṣidunī wa-tanẓuru ḥawlahā
wa-yurībuhā ramaqun wa-innī muṭmi'u
wa-taẓallu tanshiṭunī wa-tulḥimu ajriyan
wasṭa l-'arīni wa-laysa ḥayyun yadfa'u

[9] Translation of *ḥāmi l-ḥaqīqati* follows Tibrīzī, Zawzanī, etc. Arberry, *The Seven Odes* (London, 1957), 182, has "a defender of the right," which is fluent but misleading. For examples of the phrase in the *marthiya,* cf. *Anīs al-julasā' fī sharḥ dīwān al-Khansā',* ed. L. Cheikho (Beirut, 1895), 2, 11, 104. Several fine verses honoring a killed enemy are cited in 'Alī Aḥ. Sa'īd, *Muqaddima lish-shi'r al-'arabī* (Beirut, 1971), 17 and 35.

> *O the pity of it! The shaggy-maned hyena came towards me, with that limping walk of hers, as if on three legs. / All day she sat looking about her, waiting to pounce. I draw a last breath; it disquiets her, because I have aroused her greed. / She will be ripping me apart to offer my flesh to her cubs in their covert; no one alive will drive them back.*

But in the *qaṣīda* the standard answer to the problem is different. The protagonist engages in actions that are felt to be analogous to heroic death in that they are instances of relinquishment and voluntary loss. Unlimited generosity is one of these, generosity that goes beyond kindness and social bonding value and becomes a destruction of what one may need for sustenance tomorrow.

The reprover is shocked (*Muf.* 1:21, Ta'abbaṭa Sharran): *ahlakta mālan law ḍaninta bihī*, "You have destroyed your property! If only you had held on to it!"[10] The drinking scenes also belong here. They are not content to record moments of pleasure; equally essential is their testimony to the speaker's reckless willingness to spend: *fa-idhā sharibtu fa-innanī mustahlikun mālī*, "Whenever I drink, I bring ruin to my wealth."[11] Potlatch—"killing property," as the Tlingit call it[12] —is celebrated in these poems, but it is cut loose from its social moorings. To count no odds, to walk the brink and throw caution to the winds: these are the principles of the old poetry that must be remembered when its transformations after Islam are traced.

Relinquishment that can be reflected upon brings about a balance between spending and seizing, two poles well de-

[10] Reading *ḍaninta* with Anbārī and Lyall.

[11] 'Antara, *mu'allaqa*, 40.

[12] M. Mauss, *The Gift*, transl. by I. Cunnison (New York, 1967), 102, note 122.

scribed by the terms Gaster chose for seasonal rites of lean and plenty: *kenosis* (emptying) and *plerosis* (filling).[13] The Stoic, although unable to withdraw from physically registering pain and pleasure, attains an equilibrium by not permitting himself to become engaged and caught up in these sensations. The heroic model is of an equilibrium produced by the only other possible means: the will to be caught up in all encounters, joyful and lethal alike.[14]

In the poems, the reach for balance has a technical counterpart in the deployment of adjacent units of verse which together make up a thematic symmetry. This often happens with the large, traditional themes: war and peace, want and abundance, etc. It is more striking at the next level of organization. So ash-Shanfarā speaks in the poem known as *Lāmīyat al-ʿarab* of the hardships of winter and summer. Imra'alqays recalls the short final portion of a night spent in delightful company, and immediately afterwards speaks of the apparent endlessness of a night spent alone. The cheery experience took place (*muʿallaqa*, 25):

idhā mā th-thurayyā fī s-samā'i taʿarraḍat
taʿarruḍa athnā'i l-wishāḥi l-mufaṣṣali

When the Pleiades, about to set, are seen sideways in the sky, like the looped portion of an ornamental belt of cowries separated by gems.

The long night gave this impression (vs. 48):

[13] Th. Gaster, *Thespis* (Garden City, N.Y., 1961), 23.

[14] For the pre-Islamic hero's equal welcome to pleasurable and painful experiences, cf. M. Nuwayhī, *Ash-shiʿr al-jāhilī* (Cairo, without date), I, 419: *al-indifāʿ al-histīrī fī taṭallub maladhdātihā* [of life] *wat-tarḥīb bi-ālāmihā ʿalā ḥadd sawā'.*

ka'anna th-thurayyā 'ulliqat fī maṣāmihā
bi-amrāsi kattānin ilā ṣummi jandali

As if the Pleiades were hung in their station from solid rocks by ropes of flax.

Within the same section of a poem, adjacent lines may be made to balance. This is how Imra'alqays concludes his picture of a flashflood (*mu'allaqa*, 81-82):

ka'anna makākīya l-jiwā'i ghudayyatan
ṣubiḥna sulāfan min raḥīqin mufalfali
ka'anna s-sibā'a fīhi gharqā 'ashīyatan
bi-arjā'ihi l-quṣwā anābīshu 'unṣuli

It is as if the birds whistling early morning in the valley had been given an excellent wine of a lively, tinglish quality to drink; / as if, at its extremities, the beasts drowned in the late evening were wild leeks plucked from the ground.

We may turn now to the question of the relation between the tableaux of the first and second halves of the poem. Is it fortuitous that these set pieces are a standard component of the *qaṣīda*? Put starkly: should we assume that the inventory of the composite poem evolved and flourished by a survival of the structurally neatest sequences of motifs?

Since the question has to do with evolution, some historical remarks are in order. Taking a large body of ancient Arabic poetry, such as the *Mufaḍḍalīyāt*, we find that in many of the complex poems which open with a *nasīb* (the amorous opening scene), that section is followed by a detailed camel description, but only some of these poems contain a distinct block of verses devoted to the poet's journey through the desert.[15] In later times, when the *qaṣīda* was chiefly a panegyric to one's patron, the standard sequence had become *nasīb*—journey through perilous deserts to the patron's seat—praise. Such is Ibn Qutayba's recipe, in the ninth century.[16] The idea of journeying is present in the camel sections of the old poems, but it is frequently dependent on, or implied by, the camel (or horse) description; it is rarely autonomous and possessed of a specific goal.[17] The transition from *nasīb* to camel section in two poems without specific journeys will illustrate this. *Mufaḍḍalīyāt*, 38:5-6 (Rabī'a ibn Maqrūm):

fa-fāḍat dumū'ī fa-nahnahtuhā
'alā liḥyatī wa-ridā'ī sujūmā
fa-'addaytu admā'a 'ayrānatan
'udhāfiratan lā tamallu r-rasīmā

My tears overflowed, pouring down over my beard and clothes, although I tried to hold them back. / Then I turned a white she-camel away from there, one swift as a wild ass, large, never exhausted by traveling at a brisk pace . . .

Mufaḍḍalīyāt, 24:6-8 (Tha'laba ibn Ṣu'ayr):

[15] A different sampling of ancient poetry gives the same result in Jacobi, *Studien*, 12-13.

[16] Ibn Qutayba, *Kitāb ash-shi'r wash-shu'arā'* (Beirut, 1964), 20-21.

[17] A Rwala poet's camel description is an allusion to his desire to leave his uncle (Musil, *Rwala*, 362): "O uncle mine, ah, I long to saddle a thoroughbred camel on which, crossing my legs, I would go far in a day; / When I bid her drink she will drink the last drop from a small bucket, while, all around, riding camels crowd together rubbing the leather covers of their saddles. / She shies on hearing a swift flight in the hills, the flight of the *ḳaṭa'* birds, who as they rise set their eggs moving." The background story is related by Musil.

wa-idhā khalīluka lam yadum laka waṣluhū
fa-qta' lubānatahū bi-ḥarfin ḍāmiri
wajnā'a mujfarati ḍ-ḍulū'i rajīlatin
walaqā l-hawājiri dhāti khalqin ḥādiri
tuḍḥī idhā daqqa l-maṭīyu . . .

If your friend's ties to you do not endure, put an end to your need of him with a strong, trim she-camel, / solid, large in the middle ribs, fit for long treks, rapid in the midday heat, bulky; / one that continues to travel in the forenoon when the other riding beasts are weary . . .

It also occurs that the landscape through which the poet and his camel proceed receives a good bit of attention, but no destination is named; as in *Mufaḍḍalīyāt*, 26:13-19 ('Abda ibn aṭ-Ṭabīb):

idhā tajāhada sayru l-qawmi fī sharakin
ka'annahū shaṭabun bis-sarwi marmūlu
nahjin tarā ḥawlahū bayḍa l-qaṭā qubaṣan
ka'annahū bil-afāḥīṣi l-ḥawājīlu
ḥawājilun muli'at zaytan mujarradatun
laysat 'alayhinna min khūṣin sawājīlu
wa-qalla mā fī asāqī l-qawmi fa-njaradū
wa-fī l-adāwā baqīyātun ṣalāṣīlu
wal-'īsu tudlaku dalkan 'an dhakhā'irihā
yunḥazna min bayni maḥjūnin wa-markūli
wa-muzjayātin bi-akwārin muḥammalatin
shawāruhunna khilāla l-qawmi maḥmūlu
tahdī r-rikāba salūfun ghayru ghāfilatin
idhā tawaqqadati l-ḥizzānu wal-mīlu

When the company's journey grows arduous along the beaten track, which resembles a palm branch stripped of leaves, the kind woven into mats in Yemen; / along a distinct road on either side of which you can see handfuls of eggs that look like glass phials in the hollows the qaṭā-*birds have dug for them, / glass phials filled with oil and without any palm-leaf cover on them; / when, after a long journey of much exertion and no rest, little is left in the big communal water-bags and only residual moisture in the men's private water-skins, / while the last drop of stored-up strength is squeezed out of the white camels, some prodded by sticks or by the riders' heels, / some urged on gently, a little at a time, their saddles loaded on other beasts and the removable appurtenances carried by the travelers, / then a she-camel that is accustomed to being first leads the caravan, mindful of the road even as the rugged and rocky ground and the milestones grow burning hot.*[18]

The tableaux must have developed something like this: at an early period, the *nasīb* was customarily—although not always—followed by a camel description that celebrated such qualities as endurance and speed, and naturally enough contained flashes of desert journeys. The movement thus represented was not oriented towards a goal. Some poems—besides panegyrics—had autonomous sections in the *mufākhara* (praise of oneself or one's tribe) about crossing deserts; these too had no interest in the traveler's destination. To specify and stress the goal was appropriate to the panegyric. While various goals do on occasion appear in old poems (e.g. *Muf.* 47 and *Muf.* 120, where the poet travels to meet the lady), orientation towards a goal becomes standard

[18] Anbārī comments (*Muf.* I, 274): *al-mīlu mina l-arḍi maddu l-baṣar,* "*mīl,* referring to land, means *as far as the eye can see.*" Lyall (*Muf.* II, 94) translates *mile-pillars,* which I follow because Anbārī's interpretation is harder on the grammar of the original.

only with the emergence of the panegyric as the dominant type of *qaṣīda*. No such dominance can be found in the early corpus.[19]

The history of the *nasīb* is also problematic. In medieval Islamic times, poets and philologists felt that the desolate campsite motif was and always had been the proper introduction to a *nasīb*. In the pre-Islamic period, however, such was not yet the case. In al-Mufaḍḍal's collection, there are 53 composite poems beginning with the theme of a past love affair, but of these only 23 contain the campsite motif (*aṭlāl*).[20] Even so, the *aṭlāl* motif is present in nearly half our sample. Among the seven *mu'allaqāt*, there are five with and only two without, but there is just a chance that the *mu'allaqāt* are not rather extraordinary pre-Islamic works, but brilliant forgeries that stress some theatrical features in the ancient poetry. It can be safely said that the *aṭlāl* motif is the most dramatic among the various *nasīb*-themes—such as the description of parting, or a dream-visit by the lady's phantom—in that it contrasts the irreversible time of human experience with the recurrences possible in nature. The master subject of the *nasīb* is the flow of time that will not be dammed for affection; contrasting presentations of human and cyclical times set this subject in relief. Thus, in Labīd's *mu'allaqa*, what is a scene of desolation for man is also the tranquil idyll of a returning season (verses 6-7):

19 The view that the specific desert journey entered the standard *qaṣīda*-sequence when the panegyric came to pre-eminence has been already developed in Jacobi, *Studien*, 4 and 106.

20 There seems to be no correlation between the frequency of the campsite motif and the relative chronology of the 53 *qaṣīdas*. Of the 23 with campsites, 6 are by poets who lived into the Islamic period (*mukhaḍrims*) or were born Muslims. This proportion is not significantly different from the overall ratio, in the anthology, of 47 pre-Islamic poets to 20 *mukhaḍrims* and born Muslims.

fa-'alā furū'u l-ayhuqāni wa-aṭfalat
bil-jalhatayni ẓibā'uhā wa-na'āmuhā
wal-'īnu sākinatun 'alā aṭlā'ihā
'ūdhan ta'ajjalu bil-faḍā'i bihāmuhā

The ayhuqān-*branches have shot up. Antelopes and ostriches have given birth at the borders of the valley. / The big-eyed wild cows are relaxed about their newborn calves, which roam about the plain in small herds.*[21]

Moreover, the abandoned campsite is an embodiment of the nomadism that dictates the meetings and partings which the *nasīb* deals with. When we consider that the poets never write *nasībs* about their wives, but (not so much by loathing of matrimony as by convention of the genre) always choose women from whom they must be separated at last, we see what a very suitable scenario the *aṭlāl* made for a parting that the need to sustain life rendered certain.

When the *aṭlāl*-motif is present, it emphasizes the temporal and spatial relations in the opening tableaux, but these relations are there in any case. Basically, the *nasīb*'s involuntary temporal movement towards *kenosis* is paralleled by the voluntary movement without a destination, which the camel-section contains. In poems with *aṭlāl* this parallelism is staged and set out in a particularly neat manner. In the *aṭlāl*-scene, time present has no effective contents to speak of. The past has a specific burden; the present is indeterminate except by reference to a memory. The speaker arrives at a desolate but familiar spot; we are not told what business led him there. We never learn how he has spent his life since he last saw the

[21] *bihāmuhā* must refer to the calves; cf. Lane *sub voce*, with references to Jawharī and to the *Tāj al-'arūs*. It is *badal* for *aṭlā'ihā*. The translation "lambs," which is sometimes found, seems to me awkward in both grammar and meaning.

place. In this way, the emptiness at the conclusion of the affair is given a depth in time.

On the other hand, the location tends to be very determinate indeed. Place names are often mentioned. As a result, the movement without goal implied by the camel-section is the more striking for having a specific place of origin. More than that: the *aṭlāl* are the point where the temporal and spatial coordinates meet, providing a clear focus for the relations set up in the tableaux. It is not accidental that the transition from the campsite theme to the camel theme tends to emphasize renunciation as an act of will. The voluntary re-experience, spatially, of the temporal *kenosis* in which the will can have no role presents a kind of supporting paradigm to the scheme whose terms are death and voluntary loss.

Lady and camel—icons of the *nasīb* and of the camel-section—play significant roles, the contrasts between them pointing up the two principles of organization in the *qaṣīda.* First, they illustrate metaphorical re-enactment: the lady is an emblem of involuntary movement towards emptiness through time, the camel of voluntary movement towards emptiness through space. Second, they illustrate the attaining of an equilibrium by the use of contrasting pairs: the lady stands for a life of ease, the camel for stress and exertion; the one is deliciously plump, the other hard and gaunt. *Plerosis* and *kenosis.*

3

The camel description has two fairly common satellite topoi that are introduced under the guise of comparisons. The animal's tenacity and speed remind the poet of a wild ass or of an oryx, and he will often derail the simile to compose a detailed idyll about one or the other of these creatures. The wild ass is seen urging his mate up into the hills towards a privacy appropriate to the mating season. The oryx is spotted by a hunter who lets loose his hounds; they give chase; at bay the oryx turns, and gores and kills its pursuers. In some cases (e.g. *Muf.*, 40) the hounds are wary of closing in and the oryx outruns them. No doubt, ass and oryx demonstrate vaunted excellencies of the poet's camel. The tableaux in which they play their role also exhibit moods that are alien to the heroic gesture. The wild ass mates for good, in contrast with the fortuitous meetings and partings that form the theme of the *nasīb*; the hunted oryx's escape from a violent death is a reversal of the heroic seeking out of danger. In folk tales, the hero eludes the predatory ogre and gets married. In the *qaṣīda*, matters turn out so well only among animals in a state of nature. The wild ass and oryx scenes reveal, by way of contrast, the more severe fabric of the heroic model. At the same time, by establishing an opposition between the natural life of these animals and the ordered life of the hero, the *qaṣīda* implicitly confesses that the model is not a spontaneous thing but a logical construct.

4

R. P. Blackmur wrote that a mind furnished only with convictions would be like a room furnished only with light, the brighter the more barren.[22] It is a fundamental characteristic of many literary works, and even of whole genres, that they play a dialectic match with an ostensibly stable conception of life. In such masterpieces of medieval English romance as the *Morte d'Arthur* and Chaucer's *Troilus*, the mood is ironic and elegiac at the same time: the characters fall short of their own emotional models; the authors sympathize, smile, and with-

[22] R. P. Blackmur, *Form and Value in Modern Poetry* (Garden City, N.Y., 1957), 137.

hold judgment as to whether it is not the models that must in the end fail the characters.

In our *qaṣīdas,* a simple conception is often allowed to be wrecked by a simple fact. A violent death can be accommodated, but when the speaker chooses the mask of an old man looking back over his life, the organization of death and life falls apart. Old age and youth make a pair of opposites whose negative term cannot be drawn into the voluntary-loss paradigm. The peculiar poignancy of these poems stems not only from their melancholy tone, but also from the simultaneity of the elegiac and the equipoised.

The worldly philosopher is pleased by his theory of equilibrium in the universe, and feels pretty sure about it: "some like it hot, some like it cold." But sublime scenes too can employ such principles of organization. At the tranquil end of Plato's *Apology,* Socrates thinks it fair, *metriōs,* that the calumniators should live wickedly and be rewarded by shame while he dies innocent and is regarded as wise. This notion is meant to state an equilibrium; it is not maudlin resignation. Yet, here too, in the last clause, the balanced view lays itself open to question: "It is time to depart; for me who will die and for you who will live. Which of us will be better off is known to none except God."

5

The extreme conventionality, repetitiousness, and thematic limitation of the *qaṣīda* need not astonish us. To be sure, the fact that we are dealing with an oral tradition does not in itself supply adequate explanation: Homer is not so circumscribed. Other reasons must be sought for the repetitive tendency of the *qaṣīda,* and ritual is the one word that properly sums them up. H. A. R. Gibb remarked on the hieratic quality of the *qaṣīda* in the Islamic period,[23] when the genre had become, among other things, an instrument for summoning up the desert life of what was by then a time of origins, an *illud tempus.* But already in the sixth century, before the coming of Islam, these poems, rather than myths or religious rituals, served as the vehicle for the conception that sorted out the emotionally incoherent facts of life and death, and by the sorting set them at the bearable remove of contemplation. *Qaṣīda* poets spoke in affirmation of a model they shared; their poetry tended to become a shared experience, all the more as the affirmation was through the replay of prototypal events which the model so successfully charted.[24] The individual poet had considerable latitude, but individual statements were always secured by being sunk into common ground. The common ground is not a matter of conventional mood, rhetoric, or literary reminiscence, which crop up in much of European poetry too; it is the stock of specific events to which poet after poet offers himself.[25]

[23] H. A. R. Gibb, "Arab Poet and Arabic Philologist," *BSOAS,* XII (1948), 577.

[24] The notion that the *qaṣīda* grows out of collective experience is not, of course, new. Cf. Jacobi, *Studien,* 210-11. See also the following note.

[25] This requires amplification. Specific occurrences have become conventions in other literatures also. So for instance the Chinese poet loses his hat to the wind in poems about the Double Ninth festival, cf. A. R. Davis, "The Double Ninth Festival in Chinese Poetry: a Study of Variations upon a Theme," *Wen-lin; Studies in the Chinese Humanities,* ed. by Chow Tse-tsung (Madison, Milwaukee, and London, 1968), 45-64. The difference is one of quantity and complexity. The *qaṣīda* is a series of independent conventional occurrences. It is because the *qaṣīda* is a coherent complex of conventional acts that in their relationships embody the model of an order in the world that we can properly speak of ritual behavior in pre-Islamic poetry, and not be guilty of overextension. We are dealing with a particular type of ritual: it aims at affirmation and not at effecting a change, such as

The organization of material within the *qaṣīda* too has a ritualistic aspect: the series that links the tempting of death and the acts of voluntary loss consists of terms that are homological—they all have the form, or common denominator, of emptying—but not truly analogical since the terms do not all share the function of affording reflection after the act is completed. Such is the nature of what Frazer called homeopathic magic. The wooden doll and the victim share the common denominator of human shape, and the sorcerer concludes from this homology that the pinprick will bring about the desired analogical result. If the victim too is persuaded of this, he is lost. The logical leap is made convincing in the forge of ritual, or, for the pre-Islamic hero, of poetic form.

The specifically ritualistic character of the *qaṣīda* explains the curious fact that in poems composed in praise of a donor the donor's generosity is often put formulaically.[26] We must recall the verses in which war is all important, but which lack all historical particulars because war taken generically is the medium in which the heroic taken generically manifests itself. Panegyrists can apply the same formula to benefactor after benefactor, but we should be off the mark if we therefore thought all poets dissemblers and all patrons fools. The Western scholar's mind boggles at the donor's failure to be outraged upon being described by a cliché, but this is not so surprising if we consider that, according to the poem at any rate, donor and recipient engage in a ritualistic performance, acting out a segment of the total organization of experience ac-

---

stopping a toothache or a drought. That the *qaṣīda* is ritualistic is readily felt—cf. 'A. Aḥ Sa'īd, *Muqaddima*, 31: *fa-kalāmuhu 'alā mā yakhuṣṣuhu ṭaqs nafsī wa-ḥayātī wa-ta'bīrī min ṭabī'atihi an yatakarrara dā'iman*—the purpose of this chapter is to examine why the impression is sound.

[26] Several examples in Hyde, *al-A'shā*, 112, with references to 4:36-39; 5:55-58; 12:55-57 in the Cairo, 1951, edition of al-A'shā's poems.

cording to the heroic model. As long as the model holds, the donor is delighted to be moved from reality directly into the poetic rituals of heroic generosity. The poetry of modern beduins still testifies to the donor's need for a recipient. A Rweili poem ends with the curse: "Oh, may he who reviles him be parted from all that he longs for and / On festive days may no one accept gifts from him."[27]

6

The quasi-ritualistic function of the pre-Islamic *qaṣīda* accounts for an intriguing peculiarity of ancient Arabic poetics: the frequent occurrence of crowded descriptive passages. The descriptions are generally (A) static, (B) exhaustive, and (C) predictable. The modern reader is likely to find any one of these aspects a bit queer in serious verse, subscribing to Lessing's judgment that poetry has no business being pictorial. All those adjectives are fine in Annie Laurie, but Homer does not describe Helen.[28]

(A) A detailed description is static in the absence of action, and it remains static if it includes only such actions as serve to embody a quality that is being described. Thus, if in a catalogue of qualities the poet compares the lady's walk to the movement of a cloud, the result is very pretty, but not particularly dynamic. Auerbach has given an excellent example of the two types of description by putting Virgil's Camilla next to the same lady's incarnation in the Old French *Eneas.*[29] From Virgil (vii, 803-17), we learn that Camilla on foot can outstrip the winds, with a step so light that she might run over field or sea and not touch an ear of grain or a drop of a wave. Her royal attire is also taken care of, in a few glimpses.

[27] Musil, *Rwala*, 153-54.

[28] *Laokoon*, Ch. xx.

[29] E. Auerbach, *Literatursprache und Publikum in der lateinischen Spätantike und im Mittelalter* (Bern, 1958), 135-42.

All of these descriptions are worked into the movement of Camilla's arrival, past a crowd of spectators, among Turnus' allies; there is only so much portrayal as the event invites or requires. The *Eneas* poet is more than willing to stop and give us a catalogue of Camille's charms. She has a white and well-formed forehead, her head is held upright, the eyebrows are black and fine, the eyes are laughing and gay, the nose is beautiful, the face whiter than snow or ice, etc., etc. Leaving aside the question, which Auerbach is after, of the disparate expressive capabilities in Augustan Latin and early Romance vernacular, we observe that the two audiences must have placed themselves at different distances from the works they were offered. If Virgil's Camilla is perceived by the eye, the Camille of the *Eneas* poet is caressed—caressed with a great deal of respect, with grace, but caressed nonetheless. Static description—the temporary suppression of transitive action on the object's part—turns the public not into a witness (which it is in classical literature) but into a participant. It does not necessarily reduce its object into something possessible. In the Indian *Saundaryalahari*, the goddess Devi is described statically, catalogue style; but in her presence the public takes up a devotional attitude. Provisionally, let us say that static description sets off something dynamic on the part of your body: you may caress, kneel or huddle, but you do not simply look on.

(B) The descriptions tend to be exhaustive: we have catalogues of characteristics. To be sure, catalogues do not all work alike. There are menus, laundry lists, catalogues of ships, as well as lists of temples in Sumerian lamentations for destroyed cities and lists of gods, sins, and the like, in ancient incantation texts. A useful, if somewhat simpleminded, distinction can be made. A laundry list records how many of your shirts were sent out to be cleaned; a menu tells you whether there is any hope of your being served langoustines in garlic sauce. Langoustines in garlic sauce undoubtedly exist, but the menu is a restrictive catalogue, and if the langoustines happen to be in that subset of the totality of dishes that the catalogue excludes, you are out of luck. An incantation, on the other hand, wants to be comprehensive. Even if not every last member of the catalogued set receives mention, affectively such catalogues refer to a totality. To be released from suffering brought on by an unknown sin, the sufferer must go through an exhaustive enumeration of possible sins. To experience fully the pity and grief for a city razed by the enemy, the mourner composes a litany of ruined temples. Many catalogues are mixed: the Homeric listing of ships is a restrictive record as well as a source of magnitude and affective power for the poem.

The *qaṣīda* catalogues are unlike menus: they serve to render the described objects in such a way that they may be experienced exhaustively. Profiting by the tangibility that results from the static nature of description, the catalogues turn the objects into icons of the abstract relations in the model. The chief objects of description, lady and camel, through their iconic properties reinforce belief in the system of which they are a part. An important part too: we have seen that they enter both the plump/lean order, and, by the kinds of movement they summon up, the analogical voluntary-relinquishment paradigm. Mauss mentions that the Trobriand Islanders like to gaze at and stroke the objects of ritualized exchange, not so much for their intrinsic worth as for the value they derive from being tangible manifestations of the exchange system, a system of harmony.[30] Lady and camel are prized for their own sake, but in the *qaṣīda* their iconic function endows them with an aura.

[30] Mauss, *Gift,* 22. The information ultimately comes from Malinowski.

(c) As for the third characteristic, the high degree of predictability in the descriptions is quite what we should expect, precisely because each lady and each mount is a ritual object necessarily shaped to fit the grip of every member of the community.

The view that objects of detailed description function as quasi-ritualistic tokens in the *qaṣīda* gains support from a comparison of two poles of poetry in the pre-Islamic period. Poems that turn on specific events display far less static description and are far less inclined to the catalogue style than those poems which are primarily concerned with the model and which therefore refrain from specifics.[31] *Qaṣīdas* fairly often move from a non-specific first half to a conclusion that deals with a historical event; in such cases the descriptions are distributed over the halves accordingly. It may be added that descriptive verses that occur in a specific context are likely to be dynamic, being tributary to a plot. *Mufaḍḍalīyāt*, 7:5-6, Munqidh ibn aṭ-Ṭammāh:

law khāfakum khālidu bnu naḍlata naj-
jathu sabūḥun ʻinānuhā khadhimu
jardā'u kaṣ-ṣaʻdati l-muqāmati lā
qurrun zawā matnahā wa-lā ḥarimu

Had Khālid ibn Naḍla feared you, he would have been saved by a mare that at a gallop stretches her forelegs forth like a swimmer, faster than any other in the rein; / short-haired, one like a straightened spear (i.e. stretching out her neck at a full gallop), one in whose back cold weather never caused any cramps (i.e. was carefully tended) and who never suffered hunger.

[31] Already noted in Lyall, *Translations*, xx; Jacobi, *Studien*, 172, remarks on the low incidence of rhetorical devices in *qaṣīda* episodes with dramatic plots.

It is crucial to the plot that on such a magnificent animal Khālid could easily have gotten away if he had wished to flee.

As likely as not, at this point the reader will recall Annie Laurie and the fact that obviously not all descriptive blocks of verse have to do with ritualistic structures. Indeed not; and having presented my case about description in the *qaṣīda*, I must now modify my suggestions somewhat and grope towards a more general statement.

Detailed conventional description, if one is engaged neither in ritual nor in auctioneering, implies the absence of its object. *Ekphrasis*, a minute and exact portrayal—whether of a mosquito or of the Moselle river—is one thing, but the retouching of the specific into the ideal is absurd if the specific happens to be walking by your side. And indeed, in many cases the kind of movement such description triggers in the mind is an outward journey, towards a remote object. This sense of distance hangs over Annie Laurie; it is the very explicit distance of banishment that requires the loving descriptions in Kalidasa's *Cloud Messenger*.[32]

The object is rendered palpable; it is placed at a distance. Two contradictory movements: two sides of the same coin. The two can be kept apart, but they can also become confused. The palpable and the utterly remote seem two coexistent modes in those works about a Never Never Land of romantic chivalry, in which the *Eneas* poet, Spenser, and the slyer Ariosto (in Lessing's example) embraced the heresy of descriptive style.[33]

The conventional description of objects that embody and express a model of relations provides a presence. Yet, with respect to the *qaṣīda*, we must remember the undercurrent, poems of decrepitude or captivity, in which the model seems called into doubt, and in which so much is spoken from a dis-

[32] Stanza 78, etc.

[33] *Laokoon, loc. cit.*

tance (of space or time) that the nostalgic effect of description works side by side with the summoning power. This is not unduly astonishing: poetry, being a human affair, should not be furnished with certainties alone.

7

Friedrich Schlegel wrote in an early work: "Bei rohen wie bei verfeinerten Nichtgriechen ist die Kunst nur eine Sklavin der Sinnlichkeit oder der Vernunft."[34] As a judgment, this will not bear scrutiny; but it sets up a useful point of view. The old Arabic *qaṣīda* was both sensuous and logical as it faced *dahr*, time and mutability which, unconcerned with human conduct and human reason, govern the world. In a morally capricious universe, the heroic model allowed a view of the totality of experience as balanced and coherent. To achieve balance, the speaker of the *qaṣīda* offers himself to the voluntary experience of fullness as well as emptiness, of gain as well as loss. Since the experience of voluntary loss, if it is to be loss, must go beyond the socially useful, the poet who builds a model of equilibrium is compelled to represent his actions as blameworthy according to the spokesmen of the norm. It is hardly an accident that one of the consummate works of the ancient period, the *Lāmīyat al-ʿarab*, was composed by an outlaw or that, if the poem is a forgery of genius, the forger ascribed it to one.

So the method for constructing an equilibrium was somewhat roundabout, and the gate would not always be shut upon elegiac doubt. But the *qaṣīda* form, having evolved its sequence of benchmark situations, the logical relations among

[34] "With the exception of the Greeks all nations, barbarous or refined, treat art as a slave of either sensuousness or reason." F. Schlegel, *Über das Studium der griechischen Poesie* (Godesberg, 1947), 107.

them and their sensuous emblems, gave the model power of address.

wa-kharqin ka-ẓahri t-tursi qafrin qaṭa'tuhu
bi-'āmilatayni ẓahruhū laysa yu'malu
wa-alḥaqtu ūlāhū bi-ukhrāhu mūfiyan
'alā qunnatin uq'ī marāran wa-amthulu
tarūdu l-arāwī ṣ-ṣuḥmu ḥawlī ka'annahā
'adhārin 'alayhinna l-mulā'u l-mudhayyalu
wa-yarkudna bil-āṣāli ḥawlī ka'annanī
mina l-'uṣmi adfā yantaḥī l-kīḥa a'qalu[35]

I have crossed deserts bare as the back of a shield, where no traveler's beast sets foot. / I tied one end of the waste to the other, squatting or standing on a peak / while the dark yellow mountain goats come and go about me like maidens in trailing garments, / until at dusk they stand about me, motionless, as if I were a white-legged, crook-horned one, with a twist in the legs, a scaler of summits.

The old poets saw the world, even in the midst of the world, as from a mountain peak, in a glance that calmly joined shadow and light.

[35] *Lāmīyat al-'arab,* end.

two

Ghazal and *Khamrīya*: The Poet as Ritual Clown

1

Aṣma‘ī, the great eighth-century, philologist, is reported to have declared that poetry goes soft when brought into line with the Good.[1] This generalization, which springs from a discussion of the merits in Ḥassān ibn Thābit's pagan and Muslim poems, gives expression to a very sound piece of critical intuition; for Islam changed the foundations of Arabic poetry and turned the old world so thoroughly upside down that poetry was never again the same.

The change is not immediately obvious. There are many poems that clearly must have been written in the Islamic period, but hardly differ in style and spirit from works of the pre-Islamic age.[2] Still, the old conception was losing ground, however imperceptibly. A glance at the major poets of the Umayyad period is enough to persuade us that a decisive change had taken place in the poetic ethos. Social change had much to do with this: plunder and fixed stipends which the treasury paid to the conquering tribesmen at least temporarily relieved the economic insecurity that had contributed essential motifs to the old poetry. Political organization grew more complex; the sovereign importance of the individual grew more tenuous. The economic and social upheavals attendant upon successful conquest made the old beduin con-

[1] See Marzubāni, *al-Muwashshaḥ*, ed. ‘Alī Muḥ. al-Bajāwi (Cairo, 1965), 75.

[2] Cf. *Mufaḍḍalīyāt*, II, xxii-xxiii.

ception unconvincing, or at least cast doubt upon its universality.

Even aside from such matters, it is easily seen that, on the whole, heroic verse in the old style should have come to ring false. If Muslims who die in holy war are at once conveyed to Paradise and its beckoning sweets, the facing of death is no longer quite so dreadful and the challenging of it no longer quite so heroic as they had been when there was no hope of palpable reward. In short, the heroic life ceased to be a model of coherent and balanced human experience. In the relation between life and death far too radical a displacement had occurred: life and death had been two terms in opposition; they were now successive stations along a straight track to heaven or hell. The ground was cut from under the pre-Islamic *qaṣīda.*[3]

Both heroic *qaṣīda* and *qiṭʿa* (simple poem) endured because the molds were there, but their energies were ebbing.[4] It is not surprising that the three chief *qaṣīda*-poets of the Umayyad century—Jarīr, al-Farazdaq, and al-Akhṭal—put their best into a round robin of insults. Increasingly available

[3] This displacement is witnessed by the Islamic prohibition of bewailing the dead (*niyāḥa*), and of other ancient rites of mourning. Cf. I. Goldziher, *Muhammedanische Studien*, I (Halle, 1889), 251-63. *Niyāḥa*, performed by the *women*, had been the total release of a single emotion: a complement to the ordering of emotions in the heroic model. Both *niyāḥa* and heroic commemoration had now become meaningless for the Muslim, since death was no longer the end of existence, but only the end of the works for which man would be held responsible. After death the matter of Paradise or Hell was entirely in God's hands. Excessive mourning—as well as any purely human audit—was therefore a kind of impious meddling where the proper feeling was awe.

[4] For a nostalgia for the desert and the poetry associated with the desert, among the beduins who moved to Syria, see C. Nallino, *La littérature arabe des origines à l'époque de la dynastie Umayyade*, transl. C. Pellat (Paris, 1950), 110-15.

patronage required and received panegyrics, often with a political edge, but more than anything else vicious satire seems to have suited the conflicts of the day. There was no lack of conflicts, whether they lined up Arab against Arab in a struggle for power and for such benefits as would accrue to those who managed to gain important posts for their candidates, or, somewhat later, brought into the open the clash of interests between Arab Muslims and non-Arab newcomers in the Islamic community. There are enough prose descriptions of battle and of individual heroism to persuade us that a poetry with a tragic sense could have found themes in the century of civil wars.[5] Why such a poetry did not arise is not adequately accounted for by the changing attitude towards death: the *qaṣīda* proper would not work, but why did it fail to change and get a second wind? The dialectics of literary history cannot explain a non-event, and the social forces that may have inhibited the development of a tragic poetry are not immediately evident. One literary fact, though, is of obvious importance. The old heroic poetry was written in the first person singular or plural. Elegies for fallen heroes used the second or third person, to be sure, but these were not narrative poems: they aimed at ritual statement rather than the telling of a man's story. When the heroic mode of life broke up—or perhaps better, when the mode of life that allowed for a heroic image of it broke up—heroic narrative was not taken up by poetry. The heroic had been a self-image of the community; an occasional individual's fate would not now do. Such was the hold of the pre-Islamic model, and soon there was no need for a change in the treatment of heroic acts, for prose narrative jumped into the breach. Of the conflicts of the age, billingsgate in *qaṣīda* form became the proper poetic expression.

[5] Cf. the fine story of Muṣ'ab ibn az-Zubayr's death in Abū l-Faraj al-Iṣbahānī, *Kitāb al-aghānī* (Būlāq, 1868), XVII, 164.

It is symptomatic of the literary history of early Islam that the old heroic inspiration survived longest in the body of verse attributed to the Khārijites. This sect seems to have originated, around 657, among those early settlers of the Irakian garrison city of Kūfa (founded by the Arabs in or around the eighteenth Islamic year) who, lacking strong tribal affiliations, had begun rapidly to lose political and economic ground.[6] The Khārijites envisioned a puritanical, utopian theocracy that would allow the degree of anarchy—and sense of equality—available to the beduin. Their piety was real, but it was no doubt fired by the social changes that they considered a distortion of the old Muslim order.

It is not at all improbable that the poetic conservatism of the Khārijites went hand in hand with their political conservatism. But there is another matter. By the time the Khārijite poetry we still have was being written, the Khārijites had seen their religious and political hopes dissolve. Their opinions had hardened into fanaticism, and they waged holy war against one and all. Their passionate oratory was admired as much as their implacable ferocity was loathed by their fellow Muslims—whom the Khārijites refused to consider Muslims at all. Towards death the Khārijites acquired an attitude of their own. In the early days of expansion *muhājara* (emigration in order to take part in the fighting) was more or less expected of any able-bodied Muslim, but death could be regarded as a means to Paradise that was not necessarily immediately desirable. The Khārijites, on the other hand, were in the grip of a death wish: to wipe out opponents was their duty, but to attain martyrdom was their only prize.[7] Even an apparently inactive Khārijite speaks this way:

[6] Cf. M. Hinds, "Kufan political alignments and their background in the mid-seventh century A.D.," *IJMES*, II (1971), 346-67, and Nallino, *Littérature*, 182.

[7] For the Khārijite view of success and failure, cf. J. Wellhausen,

uḥādhiru an amūta 'alā firāshī
wa-arjū l-mawta taḥta dhurā l-'awālī

I fear that I might die in bed, and hope for a death under the points of tall spears.[8]

The heroic mode, whose Muse is death, subsisted among the Khārijites because among them alone death was something people chose and, in fact, lived for. They called themselves *shurāt*, "those who have sold themselves [to God]," and they kept their half of the bargain.

As we have seen, the pre-Islamic poetic manner also survived into the second Islamic century by way of forgery. It must be admitted that besides the back-door motives for such work—the antiquarian caterpillar's desire to turn into a butterfly, the preoccupation of rival tribesmen in the garrison cities with ancestral glory, and the like—the forger's art flourished because an audience for the old world-view remained. This was not necessarily an audience that harbored nostalgia for pagan conceptions; certainly it was an audience that sensed that the grasp of the old poets was more extensive and their vision nobler than anything contemporary poets could supply.

The Arab Kingdom and Its Fall, transl. M. Graham Weir (Calcutta, 1927), 65. For *muhājara* with material rather than spiritual aims, compare the line, referred to by Wellhausen (p. 25), from Abū Tammām's *Ḥamāsa*, ed. G. G. Freytag (Bonn, 1828), 792, vs. 3:

fa-mā jannata l-firdawsi hājarta tabtaghī
wa-lākin da'āka l-khubzu aḥsabu wat-tamru

You emigrated, not because you were seeking Paradise, but, as I reckon, because bread and dates were inviting to you.

A father is reproaching a son who has forsaken him in his old age.

[8] The poet is 'Imrān ibn Ḥiṭṭān. *Shi'r al-khawārij*, ed. I. 'Abbās (Beirut, 1963), 16.

The new genres that developed in the eighth century signaled that there was an inadequacy in all the aliases of the old, but also that something in the driving power of pre-Islamic verse had found a trick of metamorphosing itself.

The new poetry was not religious. In some way, Mohammed's distrust of poets—propagandists of a rival model of life—may have contributed to this. But the main reason for the voluntary exile, in this period, of poetry from religion probably lies in the comparative lack of opacity in Islam. For example, the paradoxes of Christianity were weeded out: Jesus is revered as a great prophet, but incarnation and crucifixion had to go. With religious opacity went the kind of poetic impulse that paradoxes create, and that produced some of the finest religious poetry in the European Middle Ages. Paradox jubilates in the two great hymns by Venantius Fortunatus.[9] Cosmas of Maiouma is forced by paradox into punning:

> Se ton epi hudatōn *kremasanta*
> pasan tēn gēn askhetōs
> hē ktisis katidousa en tō kraniō *kremamenon*
> thambētikōs suneikheto . . .[10]

Apart from morose, ashen, memento-mori verses, in Islam poetic response to religion belonged to the mystic. There is

[9] *Pange, lingua, gloriosi proelium certaminis*, and *Vexilla regis prodeunt*, *The Oxford Book of Medieval Latin Verse*, ed. F. J. E. Raby (Oxford, 1959), 74-75.

[10] Text in the *Penguin Book of Greek Verse*, ed. and transl. C. A. Trypanis (Harmondsworth, 1971), 432. "The Universe saw you, who without hindrance *hung* the whole earth on the waters, *hanging* upon Golgotha, and it was filled with wonder . . ." (Trypanis' translation).

plenty of mystical verse, but its vigor comes after the growth, flowering, and decadence of two secular genres: the love poem and the drinking song.[11]

The molds for such poems were present in the pre-Islamic *qaṣīda*: in the *nasīb*, and in the often encountered drinking scene. As independent genres, love poems and drinking songs came into their own only in the Islamic period. The social causes of the birth of these genres have often been discussed: the sudden rise of a somewhat languorous elegance in Mecca and Medina, cities that had grown rich with the Islamic conquests, but that lost their political weight when the Umayyad rulers shifted the center of empire to Syria; and, in the eighth century, the emergence in Baṣra and Baghdad of frivolous literary bohemians living off patronage and cultivating the novel temptations of urban life. But quite as important as social conditions are the literary conditions that furthered the development of the new genres and shaped the poets' attitudes and interests. Literary change, like linguistic change, is triggered by a variety of events—some clear, many obscure—but it follows such open lines as the original structure makes available.

If the pre-Islamic *qaṣīda* viewed human experience as absurd but coherent, the new poetry of the Islamic age —which did not choose religion for its vantage point—was forced to see human experience as meaningful under God but necessarily incoherent at the purely human level. Life had been half-mistress, half-ogre, but in poetry it had been taken as it was, and taken in its entirety. The balanced coherence

[11] For the Shī'a, the murder of 'Alī and the tragedy at Karbalā' put paradox very much back into religion. Not surprisingly, the Shī'a also acquired true religious drama. On the other hand, early Shī'ī poetry (such as the *Hāshimīyāt* of al-Kumayt) is political rather than religious.

of the old model had been achieved by a willingness to take risks, to be liberal with life as well as with money, and by a refusal to hold back. This attitude could not be shaken off, but what had been a matter of action was now translated into emotion, and a poetry of passionate but unfulfilled love—passionate inaction—was born.

It was understood to be a pernicious affection: debilitating, anti-social. This much is in the poetry. In the prose romances about great lovers—which we know from later redactions but whose growth may well have begun in the Umayyad period—the lovers pine, and pine, and in the end give up the rarefied ghost. Some go mad first. It is noteworthy that many of them are poets: the poet is still the tale's protagonist. Lovers from the Yemenite tribe of 'Udhra were said to be particularly given to such gloomy attachments, which are therefore known as 'Udhrī love. In the 'Udhrī love poem (whose authorship is by no means limited to Yemenites) everything in life is given up except the one destructive emotion: a new form of the will to *kenosis*.

In the pre-Islamic period, the poet's role was to flout norms of caution and reasonable self-interest, and through such recklessness to fashion a model for the balanced life. Under Islam, the community lived the balanced life, which Koran, prophetic tradition, and religious law mapped out between the permissible and the forbidden. The poet moved out into the margin. He was still the reckless character of the old tradition, but his function had changed. He used to provide the structure; now he evaded it. He became an actor whose best role was some form of institutionalized disorder. For this role society had a ready slot, and there we very likely have a more important social cause for the flourishing of love song and drinking song than either in the new elegance of Mecca and Medina or in the luxurious solicitations of the Irakian cities.

2

That very much of the old endures in new guises is obvious from a look at the stock vocabulary that is common to *qaṣīda*, *ghazal* (love poem), and *khamrīya* (wine song).

The familiar figure of the blamer appears in Jamīl:[12]

wa-'ādhilūna (sic) laḥawnī fī mawaddatihā
yā laytahum wajadū mithla l-ladhī ajidu
lammā aṭālū 'itābī fīki qultu lahum
lā tufriṭū ba'ḍa hādhā l-lawmi wa-qtaṣidū[13]

Blamers took me to task (lit. excoriated me) because of my love for her. If only they suffered as I suffer! / When they kept on reproaching me on account of you, I said to them: "Do not exceed the proper bounds; hold back some of this reproof and be moderate!"

[12] I am using the poems of Jamīl and Abū Nuwās as examples of *ghazal* and *khamrīya*. The type of *ghazal* represented in the works of 'Umar ibn abī Rabi'a is very charming, despite its somewhat odd narcissism, but it is less important for the main line of the *ghazal* tradition than the 'Udhrī type. 'Umar, although a city poet, seems in some ways more conservative than Jamīl: he relies more on the *aṭlāl*-motif for a curtain raiser, and his gallantry has in it a lot of skirt-chasing in the Imra'alqays manner. Admittedly, the urban features are very strong (compare the description of a letter in poem 32, in *Der Diwan des 'Umar ibn abi Rebi'a*, ed. P. Schwarz, II/2 [Leipzig, 1909], 30, which would not be out of place in the *Muwashshā*), and the parodying of religious language foreshadows a development that is still basically foreign to Jamīl. (Cf. the startling use of *a'ūdhu minki biki* in poem 91; referred to by Schwarz, IV [Leipzig, 1909], 28.)

Nallino is certainly right in seeing 'Umar as a city poet and Jamīl as non-urban, but he makes a less helpful distinction when he calls Jamīl's verse *nasīb* and 'Umar's *ghazal* (*Littérature*, 102).

[13] *Dīwān Jamīl*, ed. Ḥusayn Naṣṣār (2nd ed., Cairo, 1967), 59.

and in Abū Nuwās:

a-ʿādhilu mā ʿalā mithlī sabīlu
wa-ʿadhluka fī l-mudāmati yastaḥīlu[14]

Blamer, a person like me cannot be restrained. It is absurd of you to undertake reproving me about wine.

In the *qaṣīda*, the blamer had been a strawman of caution. His job was to try to prevent the protagonist from making the heroic gesture. Now poetry had lost heroic death as a topic, but the willingness to expose the self, to face danger and eventual destruction, retained its fascination and remained at the center by finding new forms. Paradise had spiritualized death and removed it from the arena of the heroic. The fixed idea took its place, which, whether in the form of obsession with a woman or addiction to wine, in effect meant death to all things except the object of fixation.

The lines by Jamīl are shot through with irony. The apostrophe to the blamers is in the old style. Unbridled speech is objectionable; the blamers should practice moderation, *iqtiṣād*. There are many parallels in pre-Islamic verse. But, in truth, the blamers must be accusing Jamīl of that very thing: lack of moderation. The middle way, *qaṣd*, is the way of Islam: there is even a tradition that *qaṣd*, together with deliberate and appropriate behavior (*tu'ada* and *ḥusn as-samt*), makes up one twenty-fourth part of prophethood.[15] Jamīl is

[14] *Dīwān Abī Nuwās* (Beirut, 1962), 495. Of the various uncritical editions that must be used until E. Wagner's is completed, this one (Dār Ṣādir) is most convenient. Judging by Wagner's literal translations from manuscripts, in his *Abū Nuwās* (Wiesbaden, 1965), the texts of most major poems seem reliable enough.

[15] Cf. Ibn ad-Daybaʿ, *Taysīr al-wuṣūl ilā jāmiʿ al-uṣūl* (Cairo, 1934), IV, 266.

a man who no longer feels a member of the community of men:

wa-in qultu ruddī ba'ḍa 'aqlī a'ish bihī
ma'a n-nāsi qālat dhāka minka ba'īdu[16]

If I say: "Return some of my reason that I might live with it among human beings," she says: "The chance is remote."

The very opposite of *qaṣd*. The same sense of being an outsider is found in Abū Nuwās:

adhāqanī ṣ-ṣadda sū'u tadbīrī . . .[17]

My improper conduct has acquainted me with the taste of the outcast's life . . .

Why should obsession be the mode in which walking the brink survives? As in the Greek romances, nasty turns in the lovers' separate roads to Ever After sustain the reader's interest, and consummation forever stuck *in potentia* is the first theme of the 'Udhrī *ghazal*. Such motifs have a way of inviting obsession. But there is another reason. If the spiritual refuses itself to poetry in an age that feels that human experience is tied together from above, then poetry, in its exclusion, must find human experience incoherent. Within that incoherence, obsession supplies a point of orientation.

The willingness to live one's obsession is at times obscured by the sense that fate has been at work. So for example in Jamīl's answer to a distributor of well-meaning advice:

[16] *Dīwān Jamīl*, 62.

[17] *Dīwān Abī Nuwās*, 259.

fa-qāla afiq ḥattā matā anta hā'imun
bi-bathnata fīhā lā tu'īdu wa-lā tubdī
fa-qultu lahū fīhā qaḍā l-lāhu mā tarā
'alayya wa-hal fīmā qaḍā l-lāhu min raddi
fa-in yaku rushdan ḥubbuhā aw ghawāyatan
fa-qad ji'tuhū mā kāna minnī 'alā 'amdi[18]

He said: "Sober up! How long will you be mad about Buthayna, without being able to do anything about her?" / I said to him: "Concerning her, God passed upon me the sentence that you see. Can God's decree be controverted? / Whether to love her means to be guided aright or to stray, I stumbled upon this love without intent."

At times a desire is expressed to escape from it all:

'adimtuka min ḥubbin a-mā minka rāḥatun . . .[19]

I wish I were rid of you, love. Will you leave me no rest?

To be sure, one would in no case speak of risking love as one might of risking death. But it would be a mistake to exaggerate the role of fate in the 'Udhrī *ghazal*, and then set fate against the gamble and the voluntary risk in pre-Islamic poetry. The old poetry, too, entertained a concept of fate, and its image of the heroic was capable of emotionally accommodating the paradox of risking one's fate.[20] In Jamīl's

[18] *Dīwān Jamīl*, 73-74.

[19] *Dīwān Jamīl*, 104.

[20] 'Urwa ibn al-Ward puts into verse the notion of risking fate when he speaks of gambling with the *manāyā*, the demonic powers that snuff out one's life when the time comes: *fa-in fāza sahmun lil-manīyati lam akun / jazū'an . . .*, "Should the gambling arrow of the *manīya* win, I will not lack equanimity . . ." (*Dīwān*, ed. 'Abdalmu'īn al-Mallūḥī [Damascus, 1966], 68. Incipit: *aqillī 'alayya l-lawma . . . fa-sharī*).

ghazals, the lover often complains about his destiny, but also embraces it, in an *amor amoris*:

rafaʿtu ʿani d-dunyā l-munā ghayra wuddihā
fa-mā as'alu d-dunyā wa-lā astazīduhā[21]

I have given up all desire involving this world except the love of her. Thus, I make no requests of the world, nor do I feel that I must have an ampler portion.

The following verse will help us unravel the contradictions here:

wa-qultu lahā baynī wa-baynaki fa-ʿlamī
mina l-lāhi mīthāqun lanā wa-ʿuhūdu[22]

I said to her: "You should realize that we have pacts between us, and a covenant of God."

No doubt, covenant (*mīthāq*) joins together a bundle of ideas, some fairly common in the *ghazal,* some proper to the language of the Koran. Compare the following by Jamīl:

taʿallaqa rūḥī rūḥahā qabla khalqinā . . .[23]

My soul became attached to hers before we were formed . . .

The idea in this verse reflects the scene in sura 7 of the Koran, where God challenges the yet uncreated souls of men: *a-lastu bi-rabbikum,* "Am I not your Lord?"—and the souls acknowledge God's sovereignty over them. This primordial agreement is immediately linked, in the same sura, to the covenant between God and the recipients of revelation.

[21] *Dīwān Jamīl,* 69.
[22] *Dīwān Jamīl,* 63.
[23] *Dīwān Jamīl,* 77.

It is in the nature of a covenant that it can be broken. Such is the case with the Koranic *mīthāq* too. For Jamīl, of course, there is no question of not keeping faith; nevertheless, his obsession is fate and covenant at the same time. The divine imposition of it does not rule out a parallel role for the will. Jamīl's condition is not unique: it is a trick of obsession that the victim perceives will and compulsion as coexistent.

It is in this light that Jamīl's indifference to right guidance (*rushd*) and error (*ghawāya*) must be understood. Compare the following quasi-proverbial pre-Islamic line, which is perhaps echoed in Jamīl's verse quoted on p. 42, above:

wa-hal ana illā min ghazīyata in ghawat
ghawaytu wa-in tarshud ghazīyatu arshudi[24]

What am I but one of the Ghazīya? If they err, I err; if they follow right guidance, I do too.

The poet, Durayd ibn aṣ-Ṣimma, joins his tribe in a catastrophic military engagement after the tribe has rejected his arguments for restraint. "What am I but one of the Ghazīya?" is an assent to a given situation. In the same way, Jamīl assents to the given that is his obsession, the only affiliation he admits.

Let us return to Jamīl's "I wish I were rid of you." Obsession in the *ghazal* functions as a replacement of the motif of death all the more easily as it constantly threatens to lead to death. There is no coyness or irony about the destructive power of love. When the lady's relatives complain to Marwān ibn al-Ḥakam, the governor of Medina, and Marwān outlaws Jamīl,[25] physical menace sharpens the sense of psychological

[24] Th. Nöldeke, *Delectus Veterum Carminum Arabicorum* (Wiesbaden, 1961 repr.), 32; Abū Tammām's *Ḥamāsa,* 378.

[25] Cf. Ibn Qutayba, *Kitāb ash-shi'r wash-shu'arā'* (Beirut, 1964), 347: *atāniya 'an Marwāna bil-ghaybi annahū-muqīdun damī,* etc.

ruin. It is no accident that the episode in which the government withdraws its protection from the poet and allows him to become a prey to the first comer turns out to be a folkloric motif that is also found in the biographies of a number of other *ghazal* poets.[26] Thus the cursing of Buthayna:

ramā l-lāhu fī 'aynay buthaynata bil-qadhā
wa-fī l-ghurri min anyābihā bil-qawādiḥi[27]

May God cast motes into Buthayna's eyes; may He blacken her brilliant teeth!

and the complaint that love is a prison[28] parallel the execrations, in the old poetry, of Time, in which the speaker is caught as in a current that pulls steadily towards the falls.[29]

The seriousness of his sense of doom allows Jamīl to annex the phraseology of religion with an urgency that is a far cry from 'Umar ibn abī Rabī'a's pleasantries in using Islamic expressions:

yaqūlūna jāhid yā jamīlu bi-ghazwatin
wa-ayyu jihādin ghayrahunna urīdu
li-kulli ḥadīthin baynahunna bashāshatun
wa-kullu qatīlin baynahunna shahīdu[30]

[26] Majnūn and Qays ibn Dharīḥ; see I. Kratchkovsky, "Die Frühgeschichte der Erzählung von Macnūn und Lailā in der arabischen Literatur," transl. H. Ritter, *Oriens*, VIII (1955), 27 and 46. I see no reason, however, to consider such motifs the inventions of a later age, and alien to the Umayyad *ghazal*. The wholesale ascription of romantic 'Udhrī motifs to tenth-century writers by Vadet, *L'esprit courtois en Orient* (Paris, 1968), 353-60, seems to me a case of excessive skepticism.

[27] *Dīwān Jamīl*, 53. The interpretation by Ibn al-Anbārī, quoted by Naṣṣār, is too tortuous to be credible.

[28] *Dīwān Jamīl*, 99.

[29] See Goldziher, *Muhammedanische Studien*, I, 254.

[30] This sequence of lines, found in several sources, is preferred by

They say: "Take part in the Holy War (jihād), *Jamīl, go on a raid!" But what* jihād *do I want besides the one that has to do with women? / Conversation in their company brings joy; but each man who dies in their midst is a martyr.*

Islam replaced the pagan's heroic death with martyrdom; poetry, within the fragmented experience it chose for its own, equated martyrdom with the disastrous end of obsession.

It is easy to see how such annexation of the language of Islam might imply an obsession so absolute as to leave no room for religion at all. That is the next step. Verses mistakenly attributed to writers of early 'Udhrī *ghazals* reflect the conception that a later generation of readers held of the *ghazal*—readers of a period in which the poetry of obsession had taken on an antinomian cast. An example is the line in Qālī's *Dictations*:

khalīlayya hal fī naẓratin ba'da tawbatin
udāwī bihā qalbī 'alayya fujūru[31]

My friends, is it a sin if, after having repented, I cast at her a glance to heal my heart?

whose attribution to Jamīl Qālī rightly considers groundless. Another instance occurs in the *Book of Poetry and Poets*, where Ibn Qutayba remarks that the following verse was erroneously thought to have been written by Majnūn Laylā:

yā ḥabbadhā 'amalu sh-shayṭāni min 'amalin
in kāna min 'amali sh-shayṭāni ḥubbīhā[32]

F. Gabrieli, "Ǵamīl al-'Udrī, studio critico e raccolta dei frammenti," *RSO*, XVII (1937), 71. Naṣṣār separates the two verses.

[31] Qālī, *Kitāb al-amālī* (Cairo, 1965), I, 183.

[32] Ibn Qutayba, *Shi'r*, 477.

How excellent is the work of Satan, if my love for her is of the work of Satan!

3

The incompatibility of obsession and religion, which the 'Udhrī *ghazal* usually keeps latent but occasionally lets peep out at us, becomes explicit in the wine songs (*khamrīyāt*) of Abū Nuwās.[33] These poems present life as permanent Saturnalia in which addiction has supplanted devotion. At the same time, the *khamrīya* is very much concerned with certain religious concepts and associations, and, because of the inertia of literary forms, with heroic concepts as well.

I will discuss reflections of the heroic experience, the antinomian turn of religious experience, and the assimilation of religious experience.

A. Reflections of the heroic experience

On getting drunk:

fa-ṣurri'a l-qawmu wa-stadārat
rahā l-ḥumayyā bihim fa-mālū[34]

[33] Not that there is any lack of poems, attributed to authors of the Umayyad age, in which drinking and the sinfulness of drinking are flaunted. Cf. Abū Miḥjan's verse *fa-fī shurbihā ṣirfan tatimmu l-ma'āthimu,* "disobedience reaches its perfection in drinking it unmixed," *Abu Mihǵan, Poetae Arabici Carmina,* ed. L. Abel (Leiden, 1887), 15. Some of the extraordinary shockers attributed to the Umayyad Caliph al-Walīd ibn Yazīd are collected by Mas'ūdi, cf. *Les prairies d'or,* ed. and transl. C. Barbier de Meynard and A. J.-B. Pavet de Courteille (Paris, 1861-1877), VI, 4-15. But al-Walīd's collection contains many impious verses that later opponents of the Umayyad house may very well have composed for him.

[34] *Dīwān Abī Nuwās,* 492.

The people were thrown to the ground, after the millstone of drunken giddiness had spun them around until they listed to one side.

The root ṣ-r-ʿ implies a violent movement. The turning millstone recalls the millstone of war, a cliché in pre-Islamic heroic verse. In conjunction with the phrase *istadārat raḥā* . . . , the word *qawm* will be unmistakably associated with its original sense of "fighting men of a tribe."[35]

Ibn Qutayba is not merely exercising the philologist's fancy when he discovers in Imra'alqays the pre-Islamic source of the following verse by Abū Nuwās:[36]

fī majlisin ḍaḥika s-surūru bihī
'an nājidhayhi wa-ḥallati l-khamru

In a party where joy laughs wholeheartedly and where wine is permitted . . .

Imra'alqays says this:

hallat liya l-khamru wa-kuntu mra'an
'an shurbihā fī shughulin shāghili

I am now permitted to drink wine, after having been kept from it by an all-absorbing occupation.

The occupation was avenging his father's murder; abstinence from wine (and from other amenities) was to last until blood had been shed for blood. Ibn Qutayba picks up the technical

[35] For *qawm,* cf. for instance *Mufaḍḍalīyāt* 20:17, with scholion. Abū Nuwās is expanding an old motif here. Cf. *Muf.,* 120:39b ('Alqama): *wal-qawmu taṣra'uhum ṣahbā'u khurṭūmu,* "a wine made from the juice of untrodden white grapes was throwing the men on the ground."

[36] *Shi'r,* 703. *Dīwān Abī Nuwās,* 325.

aspect of *ḥallat liya l-khamru.* It must be left undecided whether he is correct in reporting that Abū Nuwās too had a vow: to touch no drop of alcohol until he had secured a coveted rendezvous. He was no doubt justified in sensing a conscious echo—or parody—of the heroic in the *khamrīya.*

The commonplace metaphor *virgin/old woman* for old but fiery wine, as in the verse

a-mā yasurruka anna l-arḍa zahrā'u
wal-khamru mumkinatun shamṭā'u 'adhrā'u[37]

Does it not cheer you that the earth is in bloom, while
the wine is there for the taking, old and virginal?

seems to have started out as a description of war. Compare the verse by al-Kumayt:

idhā badat ba'da kā'ibin ra'udin
shamṭā'a minhā l-liḥā'u waṣ-ṣakhabu[38]

When, after having seemed a delicate young girl, war
shows itself a graying old woman, quarrelsome and
shrill . . .

Ironic punning makes use of echoes of the heroic in the following:

da' 'anka mā jaddū bihī wa-tabaṭṭali
wa-idhā mararta bi-rab'i qaṣfin fa-nzili
lā tarkabanna mina dh-dhunūbi khasīsahā
wa-'mid idhā qāraftahā lil-anbali[39]

[37] *Dīwān Abī Nuwās,* 14.

[38] *Die Hāšimijjāt des Kumait,* ed. and transl. J. Horovitz (Leiden, 1904), 98 (of Arabic text) and 70 (of translation).

[39] *Dīwān Abī Nuwās,* 499.

Put away from you toil and serious efforts [or: the things that lead to high esteem among men], and give yourself up to frivolity. If you pass a boisterous party, stop right there. / Do not commit vulgar sins. If you are going to be a sinner, then set your mind upon the noblest of sins.

Tabaṭṭal is an ambiguous word. It may mean "be frivolous" or else "act the part of the hero." "Noblest," in the second line, guarantees that this ambiguity will occur to the audience.

It also happens that a whole series of words associated with war are usurped by Abū Nuwās's preferred connotations. The flowers adorning a banquet will be our lances, the after-dinner sweet and spicy delicacies our mangonel stones, and logically enough, becoming dead drunk our killings:

fa-hādhī l-ḥarbu lā ḥarbun
tughimmu n-nāsa ʿudwānā
bihā naqtuluhum thumma
bihā nanshuru qatlānā[40]

This war is not the sort of war that grieves people by strife. / We kill people by it, and by it we revive those we have killed.

To sum up, in Abū Nuwās the borrowing of heroic language is of the brandy-is-for-heroes kind, and the borrower gives the cold shoulder to such heroism as might be sought outside the wine garden and the upstairs room.

B. The antinomian turn

The wine song's attitudes towards religion are something of a tangle.

[40] *Dīwān Abī Nuwās,* 613.

da'i l-basātīna min wardin wa-tuffāḥi
wa-'dil hudīta ilā dhāti l-ukayrāḥi[41]

Leave the gardens of roses and apples; direct your steps —may you be guided aright—towards Dhāt al-Ukayrāḥ!

No doubt, on hearing a line like this, the audience's first reaction was astonishment. "Leave the gardens" misleads you: when taken by itself, it would better suit an ascetic poem. In the next half-line the optative turns the sentence into something of a sermon. Right guidance is a frequent notion in the Koran and in pious exhortations, but the place where the spiritual pilgrim is advised to go happens to be a monastery of Christian monks who sell excellent wine. It is all a bit of a joke, and the invitation is not uncommonly outrageous: people often used to go on outings to such monasteries. The scandal is in the wording rather than in the contents. To drink wine had been forbidden by Islam, but many people did drink. In this period the outlawing of alcohol remained unenforced as often as not, and more than a few high officials of state opened a jar of wine now and then. This kind of thing went on much as in Christian Europe quite a lot of fornication must have taken place in spite of, or without accompaniment by, the roar of an already imagined hellfire. It is a fact, however, that addiction to wine was considered by the pious a great sin, *kabīra,* which would keep a man out of Paradise.[42]

The matter becomes more entangled when the speaker in the poem is conscious of breaking a prohibition of religious law and chooses to vaunt the transgression. Nothing could be more explicit than *qum sayyidī na'ṣi jabbāra s-samawāti,*

[41] *Dīwān Abī Nuwās,* 155.

[42] Cf. Ibn ad-Dayba', *Taysīr,* IV, 271.

"Come my lord, let us rebel against the Despot of Heaven,"[43] or a creed such as this:

anifat nafsiya l-ʿazīzatu an taq-
na'a illā bi-kulli shay'in ḥarāmi
mā ubālī matā yakūnu wa-qad qa-
ḍaytu minhu s-surūra ka'su ḥimāmī[44]

My proud soul will be content with nothing but the forbidden. / I do not care when my cup of death will come; I have already had my fill of the joys of the [*wine*] *cup.*

The Muslim writer who set about praising the joys of alcohol had a ready excuse: the Prophet himself declared that poets say one thing and do another.[45] The widespread doctrine that poetry has nothing to do with reality was tailored for the irreverent. But within a poem poetry has its own reality: once religion is brought in by the poet, it cannot be disengaged from other matters in the work. The world created in the *khamrīya* is not something apart from religion, *bi-ma'zil min ad-dīn.*[46] Islam had perhaps little use for poetry; poetry had much use for Islam. Therefore, in "let us rebel against the Despot of Heaven" the consciousness of rebellion really matters. With this consciousness, Abū Nuwās's wine songs pass beyond the jolly mimesis of dissipation. That there is a thrill to the forbidden was as much of a commonplace of psychology in the Middle Ages as it is now.[47] But it is not so easy to say whether the emotion described here is a delicious

[43] *Dīwān Abī Nuwās,* 117.

[44] *Dīwān Abī Nuwās,* 567.

[45] Koran 26:226.

[46] Cf. Abū l-Ḥasan al-Jurjānī, *al-Wasāṭa bayna l-Mutanabbī wa-khuṣūmih* (Ṣaydā, 1912), 58, in a passage concerning Abū Nuwās.

[47] Cf. al-Jāḥiẓ, *Kitāb al-ḥayawān,* ed. ʿAbdassalām Muḥ. Hārūn (Cairo, 1966), I, 167-68.

shudder in Mr. McGregor's garden, or something graver. "I do not care when" is of course an intentional echo of the heroic devil-may-care,[48] but it does not suffice to resolve the case. The invitation to rebel needs a closer look.

There are many instances in the *khamrīyāt* of a light-hearted knocking at hell's gate. In these passages, the poet appears a kind of ritual clown who brings a sense of release because behavior is permitted him that is not permitted others. Such is the case in most of the passages where Iblīs, the devil, is mentioned. He is at times called upon for a bit of help in a pleasantly wicked cause, because power over objects of sinful desire is the most practical among the devil's prerogatives. But anecdotes involving such matters always have a comic peripety: the devil turns an ill-starred love affair into success:

fa-raddahu sh-shaykhu 'an ṣu'ūbatihī
wa-ṣāra qawwādanā wa-lam yazali[49]

The Old Man turned him from being intractable, and became our guide, which he has been ever since.

Iblīs is never a very sinister figure: he is an arch old fellow with whom it is entertaining, and not too dangerous, to do business.

The beloved's asperity is something of a mock catastrophe. The impious intent of the wine song lies in its response to the real catastrophe, the uncertainties of time:

idhā kānat banātu l-karmi shurbī
wa-qiblatu wajhiya l-ḥusnu l-jamīlu
amintu bi-dhayni 'āqibata l-layālī . . .[50]

[48] Cf. *mā ubālī, Mufaḍḍalīyāt,* 20:31.
[49] *Dīwān Abī Nuwās,* 495. [50] *Dīwān Abī Nuwās,* 496.

> *When my drink is the daughter of the vine, and when beauty is the* qibla [*direction in which one faces at prayer*] *of my face, / I find safety in these two from the evil things that unfold with the passage of time . . .*

To a pious Muslim, the revolutions of the wheel of fortune appeared a beneficial reminder that in this world nothing endured, that nowhere except in heaven or in hell would one stop for good, and that, before attaining a permanent state, one would have to face a judgment, of whose terrifying uncertainty all other uncertainties were only a shadow. But the terror, too, was beneficial. It turned the believer away from this world and made him look to the next. The sense of safety on earth was a ruinous delusion, precisely because cocksureness about the acts of God in this world implied an arrogance towards God's final judgment, which must lead to a final calamity. The pious sound the alarm: "The world will afflict the gullible who think that they have found safety," or "You feel safe about what you have been cautioned against."[51] Fear of judgment can be overpowering: "For the believer, the grave is best of all things: he finds rest from the cares of the world and he is [as yet] safe from divine punishment."[52]

In the last-quoted lines by Abū Nuwās, the use of the word *qibla* reinforces the sense of a rival attitude: the speaker refuses to conform to proper Muslim behavior, obstinately looking for safety outside Islam.[53] Pious exhortations will do no

[51] Cf. Abū Nu'aym al-Iṣbahānī, *Ḥilyat al-awliyā'* (Cairo, 1932), II, 136; ash-Sharīf ar-Raḍī, *Nahj al-balāgha*, ed. Muḥ 'Abduh (Beirut, 1963), 225. In back of all of this is Koran 7:96-99, where the unbelievers, instead of obtaining the blessings attendant upon faith, think themselves safe from God, and invite disaster.

[52] *Ḥilya*, II, 97.

[53] The expropriation of the word *qibla* has precedents; e.g., in al-Farazdaq's panegyric to the Banū Marwān, *Dīwān*, ed. 'Abdallāh aṣ-

good; let the pious despair: *fa-shuqqī l-yawma jaybaḳi lā atūbu*, "rend your garments today, I will not repent!"[54] The blamer is now a *wāʿiẓ*, a religious warner. The poet in Abū Nuwās's *ḳhamrīyāt* becomes the exact opposite of the *wāʿiẓ*. Typically, he may choose to turn upside down the phrases that his counterpart holds particularly dear. When, for example, Abū Nuwās writes *tazawwad min shabābin laysa yabqā*, "store up provisions of youth which does not last," he plays on the often-heard reminders based on *tazawwadū fa-inna ḳhayra z-zādi t-taqwā* (Koran 2:197), "store up provisions; for the best of provisions is the fear of God."

To be fully effective, the ritual clown and the man of pious exhortation depend on one another. It is the peculiar charm of the characters later created by Hamadhānī and Ḥarīrī that they unite the two roles in a single person. Badīʿ az-Zamān's Abū l-Fatḥ himself expresses this:

sāʿatan alzamu miḥrā-
ban wa-ukhrā bayta ḥāni[55]

Now I ḳeep close to the prayer niche, now to the tavern.

Abū Nuwās makes quite explicit the willful turning away from the call of religion:

ʿāṭinī ka'sa salwatin
ʿan adhāni l-mu'adhdhini[56]

Give me a cup to distract me from the muezzin's call!

Ṣāwī (Cairo, 1936), 623, referred to by Gabrieli in *Colloque sur la sociologie musulmane* (Brussels, 1961), 290.

54 *Dīwān Abī Nuwās*, 37.

55 *Sharḥ maqāmāt Badīʿ az-Zamān al-Hamadhānī*, comm. by M. M. ʿAbdalḥamīd (Cairo, 1962), 436.

56 *Dīwān Abī Nuwās*, 595.

It is dawn; the muezzin's call reminds the drinkers that time is passing. The drinker looks for *salwa*, distraction from an anxiety. Most elegantly, a single verse reveals the shudder at the party's end, at the returning of time; the call of religion, which proclaims that with each night past time grows shorter and that man should look to what he ought most to be anxious about; and the perilous distraction chosen by the drinker: the unsafe safety of shutting his eyes upon time.

Getting drunk was no allegorical business for Abū Nuwās. But when a poet consciously defines his stance as the opposite of the pious preacher's, he just as consciously dares the public to listen to his work in full awareness of the *wā'iẓ*'s language. The word "drunkenness" had allegorical overtones for anyone who ever listened to a sermon, or a religious soapbox-oration. So had "sleep," "stupor," and the like—all stock-in-trade in the *ḵhamrīya*. For example, in a letter that Ḥasan al-Baṣrī allegedly sent 'Umar ibn 'Abdal'aziz, passion for this world is said to blind a man to what he should be concerned with, so that when the hour strikes *ishtaddat ḵurbatuhu ma'a mā 'ālaja min saḵratihi*, "his anguish is intense despite the extent to which he has managed to remedy his drunkenness," because now *ijtama'at 'alayhi saḵrat al-mawt*, "the throes of death are upon him."[57] *Saḵrat al-mawt* is the agony that deprives the sufferer of his powers of reason. The *saḵra* (drunkenness) of passion for the world was then just such a suppression of reason, and a prefiguration of an unpropitious death. In the wine poem, *saḵra* is a natural enough topic, but it is also a gesture: if it provides a kind of escape from time and fortune, that escape, for the Muslim, is as good as jumping from the frying pan into the Fire.

In discussing the invitation to rebel, we must keep in mind that there are verses in which Abū Nuwās speaks as a complete unbeliever. Ibn Qutayba quotes one of these:[58]

[57] *Ḥilya*, II, 135.

[58] *Shi'r*, 691.

ḥayātun thumma mawtun thumma ba'thun
ḥadīthu khurāfatin yā umma 'amri

Life followed by death followed by resurrection—all that, O Umm 'Amr, is an old wives' tale.

It is very simple and straightforward, but it may be a literary pose. After all, Abū Nuwās also wrote ascetic poems and poems that implore divine forgiveness. We might assume that he found repentance in old age, after riotous decades throughout which he had held the very idea of another life in contempt, but there is good reason to think otherwise. We see from biographical details reported by a variety of authorities that in Abū Nuwās extreme impiety, repentance, and recidivism could quickly follow one after the other. There is an enlightening anecdote.[59] Abū Nuwās and some companions are on a drinking excursion and are having a jolly time when a cloud of piety abruptly settles over some of the drinkers, who remind Abū Nuwās of the dreary prospect of divine punishment. If there is one thing Abū Nuwās cannot stand it is a spoil-sport, and he answers:

mā ṣaḥḥa 'indī min jamī'i l-ladhī
tadhkuru illā l-mawtu wal-qabru

Of all you have been saying, I find only death and the grave indubitable,

which, not surprisingly, horrifies his companions. To deny the resurrection is not at all of the same order of sinning as to wet one's throat on a fine day.[60] Reproved by his friends, Abū

[59] al-Khaṭīb al-Baghdādī *Ta'rīkh Baghdād* (Beirut, 1966), VII, 441-42; Abu Hiffān al-Mihzamī, *Akhbār Abī Nuwās*, ed. 'Abdassattār Aḥ. Farrāj (Cairo, 1953), 36-38. *Ta'rīkh* prints *tadhkuruhu* in the verse below, which does not suit the meter (*sarī'*).

[60] Cf. *al-Adab aṣ-ṣaghīr*, attributed to Ibn al-Muqaffa', in *Rasā'il al-*

Nuwās recants and apologizes. He holds no faith but Islam; however, *rubbamā nazā bī l-mujūnu ḥattā atanāwala l-ʿaẓāʾima wa-mā aʿlama annī masʾūlun ʿanhu wa-muʿadhdhabun ʿalayh*, "from time to time *mujūn* (libertinism, frivolity) overcomes me to such an extent that I commit mortal sins, oblivious of being answerable for it (*mujūn*) as well as of the punishment that it will bring upon me." This is followed by an extempore poem—it turns out to be one of his most famous in the ascetic genre—and after that is over, all go back to do some more drinking.

Abū Nuwās's explanation is believable. Denial of resurrection is the logical extreme of the attitude that governs the wine song. The poetics of obsession or addiction in the place of supernatural coherence at last deny supernatural coherence altogether. The position swings out this far: as far as it can go. Then it swings back to the utmost piety and the ascetic mode. What we see in Abū Nuwās is a willful failure to heed call and warning; we cannot consider his *k̲hamrīyāt* products of a mind for which the call is fatuous and the menaces of the Koran a fiction.[61]

---

bulaghāʾ, ed. Muḥ. Kurd ʿAlī (Cairo, 1946), 25: *al-muʾminu bi-shayʾin mina l-ashyāʾi wa-in k̲āna siḥran k̲hayrun mimman lā yuʾminu bi-shayʾin wa-lā yarjū maʿādan*, "A man who believes in something, even if it is black magic, is better than a man who believes in nothing and expects no resurrection."

[61] Besides the pious *zuhdīyāt*, there are also wine poems in Abū Nuwās's dīwān that treat divine judgment as a reality. For example, *Dīwān Abī Nuwās*, 544:

> la-ʿamrī la-in lam yaghfiri l-lāhu dhanbahā
> fa-inna ʿadhābī fī l-ḥisābi alīmu

Upon my life, if God does not forgive sinning with it [*wine*], *my punishment, when the accounts are settled, will be a painful one.*

Admittedly, in this period many people put on an air of frivolity in

Rather, the deportment in these poems is what C. S. Lewis called a truancy,[62] but it is a truancy acted out with much seriousness. Some comparisons will help. "My proud soul will be content with nothing but the forbidden" is not like the good-humored admissions of vice familiar from medieval European literature. When the Archpoet writes *implico me vitiis, immemor virtutis, / voluptatis avidus magis quam salutis*,[63] he reminds us of Abū Nuwās's companions, every one of whom "puts worldly things well ahead of religion," *qad āthara d-dunyā 'alā dīnihi.*[64] But the Latin poem is all fun: one sins because *res est arduissima vincere naturam*, because it is terribly hard to get the upper hand over nature, and not because one desires to rebel. And, to be sure, the Archpoet finishes with *iam virtutes diligo, vitiis irascor*, "already now I prize virtue and frown upon vice." We are not quite convinced (he does not seem to want us quite convinced), but there it is.

We also have Aucassin, who wants to go to hell with the fine knights who have perished at tourneys and with the fine,

---

religious matters because such frivolity was considered elegant; cf. Aḥ. Amīn, *Ḍuḥā l-Islām* (Cairo, 1946), I, 152-56, and G. Vajda, "Les zindiqs en pays d'Islam au début de la période abbaside," *RSO*, XVII (1937), 210, note 1. The purpose of this chapter is to demonstrate that the Nuwasian *khamrīya*'s attitude towards religion is more profound and more complicated than mere elegance and wit would have it be. I must stress that I am concerned with the attitudes explored in Abū Nuwās's wine songs; whether the historical Abū Nuwās shuddered every time he thought of the Last Judgment, or, quite the opposite, entertained some form of Murji'ite doctrine with particularly sanguine expectations of divine forgiveness, it is impossible to say.

[62] C. S. Lewis, *The Allegory of Love* (New York, 1958), 104.

[63] "I get all tangled up in vice; I forget virtue; I crave pleasure more than salvation." *The Oxford Book of Medieval Latin Verse*, 264.

[64] *Dīwān Abī Nuwās*, 600.

courtly ladies who have two or three friends besides their husbands, but this is a raving answer to the reprimand that hell would be his lot if he became Nicolete's lover.[65] Troilus, too, is forgetful: *All other dredes weren from him fledde, / Both of th'assege* [= siege] *and his savacioun,*[66] but once again, Abū Nuwās's "Come let us rebel" is a different matter.

The invitation to rebel has melancholy for a backdrop. "Do not stop to question desolate encampments that will yield no news of their vanished inhabitants," we read again and again, "better reach for the cup." The inversion of the *aṭlāl* motif is a literary game, but it is also more than a game. The old balances are gone now: the theme of departure and of abandoned places, however ironically put, conjures up loss and futility, which leave a shadow, even after the poet has gone on to more exhilarating topics. As an example of such openings, here is a verse in which the symmetry of consonants joins together grief and solace:

lā taḥzananna li-furqati l-aqrāni
wa-qri l-fu'āda bi-mudhhibi l-aḥzāni[67]

Do not grieve over the dispersal of companions;
entertain your heart with what causes sorrows to pass.

A bit of gloom over the brevity of life and the toyings of fortune often is the mood of *ergo bibamus* poetry; the combination of rebellion with the movement from melancholy to utter absorption in pleasure sets the Nuwāsian *khamrīya* apart. It is a peculiar combination of the heart's folly, the heart's boldness, and the heart's ambivalent knowledge of itself as flesh.

[65] *Poètes et romanciers du Moyen Age,* ed. A. Pauphilet (Paris, 1952), 457. Cf. the note, by Pauphilet, on the *vocabulaire violemment pittoresque de ce jeune fou.*

[66] Chaucer, *Troilus and Criseyde,* I, 463-64.

[67] *Dīwān Abī Nuwās,* 611.

There result from it a seriousness and an esthetic dignity that none of the components would attain by itself.

C. The assimilation of religious experience

The borrowing of terms and images associated with a specific mode of experience and their application to an utterly different mode may signal a variety of intents. When one mode is standard and the other something of a pariah, such borrowing may be a half-willing acknowledgment by the outsider of the *mana* in the dominant order's phraseology. The complex political structures of New York street gangs used to be an example of this. Borrowing may be a cynical leveling of the values in the dominant order, aiming to set the dominant against the outsider's mode in an even match. In turn, as when the Beatrice of the Commedia is both the Beatrice of the *Vita Nuova* and the Sapientia of the *Convivio,*[68] it may be an expression of the kind of synecdochic experience that follows upon perceiving that a mode may be inferior and yet reflect the lineaments of the superior: an experience of correspondence that brings delight and a kind of hope. Borrowing may remind us that a game is afoot, with rules that parody the rules of something serious. It can be gently or quite finger-waggingly ironic. It is with such a gently ironic hint that Chaucer quotes Dante, transferring to Cupid the homage originally offered the Virgin Mary (*Troilus and Criseyde,* III, 1261-63):

> Benigne Love, thou holy bond of thinges,
> Who-so wol grace, and list thee nought honouren,
> Lo, his desyr wol flee with-outen winges.

Against the background of *Paradiso,* XXXIII, 13-15:

[68] Cf. C. S. Singleton, "Dante: Within Courtly Love and Beyond," in *The Meaning of Courtly Love,* ed. F. X. Newman (Albany, N.Y., 1968), 43-54.

Donna, sei tanto grande e tanto vali
che qual vuol grazia ed a te non ricorre
sua disianza vuol volar senz' ali.

Lady, you are so great, and of such worth, that if anyone
would have grace and does not take recourse to you,
his desire wishes to fly without wings.

Such echoes can also be found in poetry with a carnevalesque cast: poetry in which the lowest farce prepares the highest solemnity. The Towneley *Secunda Pastorum*—surely a single author's work—is a perfect example. Not only does the farce of the stolen sheep found in the crib parallel the subsequent visit of the shepherds to the infant Jesus; the very words are repeated. Sheep and *derlyng dere, full of godhede* are both addressed as *lytylle day-starne* (morning star).[69] This is not mere play to a gallery of provincial snickerers. To give the devil his due is perhaps needed before the angelic can find room in the mind, certainly in a man who regards himself as a mixture of quite easily identifiable dross and a somewhat vaguer something else.[70]

Let us return to "Direct your steps—may you be guided aright—to Dhāt al-Ukayrāḥ" (p. 51) and take off from there again.

The wine is bright enough to guide the traveler in the dark:

[69] *Secunda Pastorum*, vss. 577 and 727: *The Wakefield Pageants in the Towneley Cycle*, ed. A. C. Cawley (Manchester, 1958), 58 and 62.

[70] Cf. the interesting observation in E. C. Parsons and R. L. Beals, "The Sacred Clowns of the Pueblo and Mayo-Yaqui Indians," *American Anthropologist*, XXXVI (1934), 503, on ritual clowns who as a rule act contrary to the norm and are called *Fariseos* and the like, but during Lent serve as guardians of the image of Christ and as his special servitors.

fa-htadā sārī ẓ-ẓalāmi bihā
ka-htidā'i s-safri bil-'alami[71]

In the gloom, the voyager takes guidance from it, as travelers might be guided by a signpost.

It did not take a fresh eye to see the shimmer of wine; al-A'shā and al-Akhṭal already compared wine to luminous objects of various sorts.[72] But Abū Nuwās brought along something that struck people as new. Ibn Qutayba certainly thought so, and quoted several examples:[73]

fa-qultu lahū taraffaq bī fa-innī
ra'aytu ṣ-ṣubḥa min khalali d-diyāri
fa-kāna jawābahū an qāla ṣubḥun
wa-lā ṣubḥun siwā ḍaw'i l-'uqāri
wa-qāma ilā l-'uqāri fa-sadda fāhā
fa-'āda l-laylu maṣbūgha l-izāri

I said to him: "Do me a favor; I already see morning in the spaces between houses." / He answered: "Morning? There is no morning except the light of the wine." / He got up and stopped up the wine jug; night returned in its dark-dyed cloak.

or

[71] *Dīwān Abī Nuwās*, 537.

[72] Their passages dealing with wine are collected in the back of I. Ḥāwī, *Fann ash-shi'r al-khamrī wa-taṭawwuruhu 'inda l-'arab* (Beirut, 1970). See also I. Kratchkovsky, "Der Wein in al-Aḫṭal's Gedichten" *Festschrift G. Jacob*, ed. Th. Menzel (Leipzig, 1932), 146-64.

[73] *Shi'r*, 692-93. *Dīwān Abī Nuwās*, 247 (with insignificant variants) and 146.

ḥasbī wa-ḥasbuka ḍaw'uhā miṣbāḥan . . .

Its light will do as a lamp for both of us . . .

The self-sufficient source of light, to which men are guided, has Islamic overtones. Cf. Koran 24:35:

> al-lāhu nūru s-samawāti wal-arḍi; mathalu nūrihi ka-mishkātin fīhā miṣbāḥun; al-miṣbāḥu fī zujājatin; az-zujājatu ka-annahā kawkabun durrīyun yūqadu min shajaratin mubārakatin, zaytūnatin lā sharqīyatin wa-lā gharbīyatin, yakādu zaytuhā yuḍī'u wa-law lam tamsashu nārun; nūrun 'alā nūrin; yahdī l-lāhu li-nūrihi man yashā'u.
>
> *God is the light of the heavens and of the earth. His light is like a niche that holds a lamp, the lamp being in a glass that seems a brilliant star. It is kindled from a blessed tree, an olive that is neither of the East nor of the West, whose oil almost radiates light even without a touch of fire. Light upon light, God leads to His light whom He will.*

The gloom through which the voyagers make their way to the bottle is, naturally enough, the other side of the *light/dark* opposition that occurs in the Koran time and time again.[74] I suspect that it was the symbolic pull of the light-imagery in Abū Nuwās's *khamrīyāt* that made Ibn Qutayba feel that there was something new in these poems. He must also have noticed a revealing change in emphasis between the old and the new: al-A'shā and al-Akhṭal occasionally spoke of the luminosity of wine, but they stressed its fragrance, while Abū Nuwās is far more interested in the play of light.

[74] Many examples collected in Vajda, "Les zindiqs," 227, Notes 3 and 4.

It is essential to note that Abū Nuwās's *khamrīyāt* also make use of imagery with religious associations whose sources must be sought outside of Islam. In some cases he is indebted to gnostic thought, the great well of cosmic images, which appears to run low with the passing of the formal Manichean religion, only to surge up again, inexhaustible, in the Ismā'īlī and Illuminationist systems. In Abū Nuwās's time, Manicheanism was persecuted; it was not yet extirpated. The majority of Muslims, presumably, had at best a garbled notion of Manichean doctrine, but it is inconceivable that poets lacking in pious scruple would at this religiously turbulent period remain unacquainted with some amount of gnostic imagery. Abū Nuwās himself reports that, in the prison where Manicheans were held and where he was taken by mischance, an acquaintance of his, Ḥammād 'Ajrad, surprised him by being unmasked as a writer of Manichean hymns.[75]

An example of reflections of gnostic imagery is the following:

isqinīhā sulāfatan
sabaqat khalqa ādamā
fa-hya kānat wa-lam yakun
mā khalā l-arḍa was-samā
ra'ati d-dahra nāshi'an
wa-kabīran muharramā
fa-hya rūḥun mukhallaṣun
faraqa l-laḥma wad-damā[76]

[75] *K. al-aghānī*, 13:74. I stress that I am speaking of imagery, not of familiarity with doctrine. Cf. the doctrinal confusion in the satire in which Abū Nuwās accuses Abān al-Lāḥiqī of being a Manichean, al-Jāḥiẓ, *Ḥayawān*, 448-50. Reference in Ch. Pellat, *Le milieu Baṣrien et la formation de Ǧāḥiẓ* (Paris, 1953), 220.

[76] *Dīwān Abī Nuwās*, 541.

> *Give me a fine wine to drink, of a vintage from before the creation of Adam, / a wine that existed when nothing was except heaven and earth, / that watched time grow up and grow old and decrepit / while it in turn became a liberated spirit that has parted from flesh and blood.*

The spirit freed of the body after eons of time, the beginning of this process before the creation of man—these are echoes of the gnostic drama. The words *rūḥ* and *mukhallaṣ* together even strike one as technical terms. According to Shahrastānī, the Manicheans will have it that the world was created to compass "the liberation of the various types of light from the various types of darkness," *li-takhalluṣi ajnāsi n-nūri min ajnāsi ẓ-ẓulma*. As it turns out, *rūḥ* is the subtlest of the *ajnās an-nūr*.[77]

Christian ceremony is perhaps in back of another mischievous passage:

> mā dhuqtuhā qaṭṭu aw unājī
> amāmahā l-ka'sa bil-kalāmi[78]

> *I have never tasted it without first whispering, in its presence, a quiet prayer over the cup.*

I do not mean to belabor the various religious echoes in the imagery of the wine song. There is no point in looking for

[77] Shahrastānī, *Kitāb al-milal wan-niḥal*, ed. W. Cureton (London, 1846), 191 and 189.

I would like to note, in passing, that while proper Manicheans drank no wine, they were not averse to speaking of wine symbolically. The pitch-covered wine jar with fragrant wine inside is described in *A Manichean Psalm-Book*, ed. and transl. C. R. C. Allberry (Stuttgart, 1938), 220.

[78] *Dīwān Abī Nuwās*, 546. The motif of prayer before wine occurs in al-A'shā, where the person who guards the wine does the praying. See *Dīwān al-A'shā l-kabīr*, ed. M. M. Ḥusayn (Cairo, 1950), 293.

doctrine; what matters is the presence of such elements in the central myth (or mime) of the *khamrīya*: the quest of a small company, in the obscurity of night, for the luminous, often also primordial, object towards which they are drawn.[79] As I. Ḥāwī observes, the wine in these poems comes very close to the mystic wine of later Sufi poetry.[80]

Imagery with transcendental associations creates in the *khamrīya* a sense of something like a rival religion. Such a development is perhaps natural enough in a religious society, but it is ironic; for it is the end of the line for a genre that sprang from a poetic refusal to accommodate to the religious model of human experience. The wine song fosters its myth; it is never quite free of the shadow of Islam.

As a result, Abū Nuwās's *khamrīyāt* contain an unresolved contradiction that occasionally finds expression. The most explicit instance is the use of *istighfār*, the begging of God's mercy, as a closing topos:

fa-dhāka qabla nuzūli sh-shaybi 'ādatunā
lākinnanā nartajī ghufrāna ghaffāri[81]

Such is our habit until our hair turns gray, but we hope for the forgiveness of a forgiving one.

A curious, elegiac contradiction occurs in poems that begin on a note of contempt for the traditional halt at a deserted

[79] The night journey, by itself, might be a parody of a heroic motif. On the heroic night journey (*idlāj*), see M. Bravmann, "The Return of the Hero; an Early Arab Motif," *Studia orientalia in honorem C. Brockelmann* (Halle, 1968), 21. The habit of inserting a circumstantial clause about the darkness or time of night (e.g., *wal-laylu mu'takirun*, *Dīwān Abī Nuwās*, 7) certainly derives from heroic poetry; cf. *Mufaḍḍalīyāt* 1, 465 (*wal-laylu dāmisu*) or *Lāmīyat al-'arab* vs. 56 (*wal-laylu alyalu*).

[80] *Fann ash-shi'r al-khamrī*, 258. [81] *Dīwān Abī Nuwās*, 261.

encampment, but end by quoting a line of verse that presents the same encampment motif, or some related beduin-style form of nostalgia and remembrance. A striking example is a poem in which there are not one but two dragons biting their own tails: it begins with the trick of keeping away a queasy awakening by taking another drink

da' li-bākīhā d-diyārā
wa-nfi bil-khamri l-khumārā

Leave the desolate dwellings to the one who will cry over them, and stave off hangover by drinking more wine,

and it ends with the verses

rafa'a ṣ-ṣawta bi-ṣawtin
hāja lil-qalbi ddikārā
ṣāḥi hal abṣarta bil-khī
tayni min asmā'a nārā[82]

He raised his voice in a tune that roused the heart to remembrance: / "O my friend, did you see in al-Khītān a fire belonging to Asmā'?"

The poem has to end somehow. Wary of a nasty morning after, it sinks deeper into poetry: it admits through the staging that the play will not really do as a model for reality.

At times, the contradiction is worked into the vocabulary. This is the case in *'afā l-muṣallā*, discussed in Chapter IV. Another example is the poem that, in verse two, describes the young men as

anḍā'i ka'sin idhā mā l-laylu jannahumū
sāqathumū naḥwahā sawqan bi-iz'āji

[82] *Dīwān Abī Nuwās*, 245.

Emaciated for love of the cup; whenever the night conceals them, they are anxiously drawn towards it . . .

and concludes with

wad-dahru laysa bi-lāqin sha'ba muntaẓimin
illā ramāhu bi-tafrīqin wa-iz'āji[83]

Time never finds people in any [group] that fits well together but that it afflicts them with separation and anxiety.

The repetition of *iz'āj* (to worry, make anxious), in a different and more serious application, determines the direction of the poem.[84]

[83] *Dīwān Abī Nuwās,* 136-37. The use of internal echoes of this kind, which is a favorite device of Abū Nuwās's, will be further discussed in Chapter IV.

[84] Both the technique and peripety of the poem have a most interesting precursor in *Mufaḍḍalīyāt,* 9, composed by Mutammim ibn Nuwayra. Mutammim's section on wine ends with the line (vs. 30)

alhū bihā yawman wa-ulhī fityatan
'an baththihim in ulbisū wa-taqanna'ū

I take pleasure in it, and with the pleasure of it distract the young men from their sorrows, if they are clothed and veiled *in sorrow.*

The metaphorical veiling (*taqanna'ū*) turns concrete and unavoidable in the last line (vs. 45):

wa-la-ya'tiyanna 'alayka yawmun marratan
yubkā 'alayka muqanna'an lā tasma'u

And once there will come upon you a day of weeping over you, when you will be shrouded *and will not hear.*

In a poem that does sound as if it had been written in old age,[85] the night journey to the wine seller's house is described like this:

fī faylaqin lid-dujā kal-yammi multaṭimin
tāmin yaḥāru bihī min hawlihi n-nūtī

Encompassed in gloom that was like a rough sea with clashing waves in which the mariner is stunned by terror . . .

In the next line, the drinkers stand in front of the wine seller herself: *idhā bi-kāfiratin shamṭā'a*, "And suddenly there was a graying woman, an unbeliever. . . ." Sura 24 again comes to mind, this time verses 39-40, in which the works of the unbeliever are compared to just such a dark, tumultuous sea. Now the poem gets down to business: the wine radiates light; it showers sparks the way angels hurl stars at rebellious demons; the saki possesses all the charm of the angel Hārūt; in the pleasure garden the strings play their music and they are like a heavenly sphere turning round and round with the drinkers. All this was long ago. Youth is past, and so the poem ends this way:

ad'ūka subḥānaka l-lāhumma fa-'fu kamā
'afawta yā dhā l-'ulā 'an ṣāḥibi l-ḥūti

I call upon you, my God, glory be to you; forgive as you, most High, forgave the man of the Whale.

Jonah takes us back to the first tempest at sea in the poem: the metaphor in line six, which gave the quest its weather. Through this short-circuit, the begging for mercy in the last

[85] *Dīwān Abī Nuwās*, 111-13.

line is pitched against the quest myth itself. The contradiction between role and reality is made explicit: the poet comes out of the Whale.

4

The heroic model bequeathed upon the *khamrīya* two characteristics from which the libertine poet was never to escape: the emphasis on the tempting of personal catastrophe—which was now a catastrophe for all eternity—and the poetic stance of being an object of reproof among the reasonable. The balance, which in the old *qaṣīda* these characteristics helped achieve, the wine song could not inherit. In pre-Islamic poetry, the heroic gesture was a peremptory social need and constructed a model for the entire community; the gesture in the *khamrīya* answered the subordinate need of institutionalized rebellion, the poet and his companions becoming a band of outsiders.

The rebellion, which comes to transcend mere *gouffre* and takes the form of an inchoate rival religion, stands heir to the ritualistic qualities of the heroic *qaṣīda*. The chief tableaux in Abū Nuwās—the night journey, the opening of the wine, etc.—retain various conventions of drinking scenes in the *qaṣīda*.

In some ways, however, the *khamrīya* makes an odd inheritor. The tavern scene is contrary to the archaic *nasīb* in that the pre-Islamic poets used to recall a full past in a vague present, while the *khamrīya* poet sees the party in the tavern as the very moment for which the wine has been stored since time immemorial: for him *now* is when the various predestined parts of the experience find one another. The contrast lies, to some extent, in the nature of the subject matter, but it is characteristic of the thoroughly different results that, in *qaṣīda* and *khamrīya*, similar poetic stances bring about.

In the *qaṣīda*, losses are voluntarily taken and danger is courted, and the result is a balance and an emotional security. In the *khamrīya*, disaster is tempted through a willful search for a false security from time, and the result is one half of a balance: the role of the ritual clown. The other half is the law-abiding Muslim. In the *qaṣīda*, elegiac overtones were a breach in the model; in the *khamrīya* they are bridges back to the extant model of coherence, to life in harmony with religious law. In sum, the *qaṣīda* chooses to see time as the plane upon which *plerosis* and *kenosis* balance each other, but the *khamrīya*—in its search for the wrong safety, in this truancy that is also a strange metamorphosis of the heroic gesture—pretends that time can be reduced to the precarious span in which obsession has its fling. Struggling not to notice the flow of time, the poetry takes on a character of constant, feverish agitation. It does so also because it must not look back and resign its role as a means of evasion; and it does so all the more easily because, as a poetry of obsession, it finds agitation its natural mode. Once again the obsessed man both wills and is trapped by his compulsion.

That the libertine subdues time is spelled out in some of the poems. Here is the beginning of the piece that ends with the whale:

wa-fityatin ka-maṣābīḥi d-dujā ghurarin
shummi l-unūfi mina ṣ-ṣīdi l-maṣālīti
ṣālū ʻalā d-dahri bil-lahwi l-ladhī waṣalū
fa-laysa ḥabluhumū minhū bi-mabtūti[86]

Young men, brilliant as lamps in the dark, all haughty, stiff-necked and keen, / who overpowered Time with the

[86] In this context, as far as I can see, *dahr* and *zamān* are used indiscriminately; cf. *dāna z-zamānu lahum, Dīwān*, 7; *dhallat lanā riqābu d-duhūri, Dīwān*, 275. Note the assonance, supporting the linkage of meanings, between *ṣālu* and *waṣalū.*

pleasures they embraced, so that the ties between them and their pleasures remained unsundered ...

But this comes from a poem in which time passes and old age arrives: the triumph over time is put most explicitly where in the end it is acknowledged as a delusion. This need not surprise us; we have seen that the *khamrīya* is a genre of contradictions.[87] In any case, the pre-Islamic drinker starts out without wild hopes about time, a contrast that a verse by al-Aʿshā makes adequately clear:

fī fityatin ka-suyūfi l-hindi qad ʿalimū
an laysa yadfaʿu ʿan dhī l-ḥīlati l-ḥiyalu[88]

Among young men like Indian blades, who had learned that the man of cunning is not protected by his stratagems [that he too must die] ...

5

In the *qaṣīda*, conventional description made palpable certain objects that embodied aspects of the heroic model. To some extent, in the one half of a model, which the *khamrīya* is, the ritualistic function of description survives. The chief objects are wine and boys: the great conventional catalogue is no longer common; but such objects are often sketched in phrases that are conventional enough to contain no information at all. Such phrases act by their presence alone. In pre-Islamic poetry the vocabulary is so much richer that it is the conventionality of the denotations that strikes us, rather than

[87] The same immediate contradiction of the triumph over time occurs in *Daʿ ʿanka lawmī . . . ighrāʾu* (*Dīwān*, 7-8), where wine goes round among young men to whom time is subservient, but in the next line the poet weeps because that wine is a thing of the past.

[88] *Dīwān al-Aʿshā l-kabīr*, 59.

the exact phrasing, even though stock phrases do occur. In the *khamrīya,* conventional description is very often reduced to basic building blocks: moon-faces, reed-waists, pearly teeth and ruby lips. Spenser too gives us ruby lips and pearly teeth, as does Ariosto, but their poetry, however decorative, is not nearly so weighed down by such descriptions as the Arabic lyric. In later Persian poetry, as Ritter has shown, the rubies and pearls become names for the objects they once described, and it is the objects that interact.[89] In Abū Nuwās this is not yet the case. "His forehead is like the crescent moon" is a predication in its own right—a simile rather than ossified metaphor—no matter how little real information we can distill from it.

Undeniably, a great deal of Abbasid poetry must have been composed extempore, and we may be tempted to explain away the moon-faces as so much stuffing.[90] The fact is, however, that such conventions crop up in poems that were obviously made with great care and attention to wording and structure. We must also not forget that whatever the way in which a convention gets into a line, once it is there it will have some sort of an effect on the mind of the audience, and the critic must attempt to pin down that effect.

As a first step, we must distinguish between the type of formula described by Parry and Lord, and the type we are interested in. In Homer, or in the Serbo-Croatian epic, formulas are operative. A formula like "Yallah, he said, and got

[89] H. Ritter, *Über die Bildersprache Niẓāmīs* (Berlin-Leipzig, 1927), 29. Cf. also Dámaso Alonso, "Poesía arabigoandaluza y poesía gongorina," *Al-Andalus,* VIII (1943), 138.

[90] For extempore composition, cf. *K. al-aghānī,* III, 129, where Abū l-'Atāhiya declaims at the potter's wheel while the young literati copy down his verses on potsherds. Also *Aghānī,* III, 131, where Abū l-'Atāhiya avers that he could speak in verse all day long if he so wished.

on his horse"[91] carries a narrative forward, and it tells us just enough of the action to suit that purpose. The same I think is true of the longer Homeric formulas. The Arabic formulas in question—"Her teeth are like camomile flowers," "Her waist is like a reed"—do not carry anything forward. They are pure description for description's sake. One might think of the permanent epithets in Homer, but those epithets are in reality names or parts of names. A phrase $x(y)$ where x is a permanent epithet will be part of some information with $x(y)$ as the subject, object, or some such. In the Arabic, we have a statement $y = z$, where the entire predication is a cliché. In the Iliad it is extremely rare that a simile is repeated.[92]

A metaphor ends its life by becoming a name, but a new simile or metaphor gives the listener the shock of a re-ordering of experience. The listener suddenly becomes the nexus of the terms of comparison. In this way the simile can function as a kind of motor for the work Heidegger attributes to the language of poetry: *Es lädt die Dinge ein, dass sie als Dinge die Menschen angehen.*[93] But repetition works changes

[91] A. Lord, *The Singer of Tales* (Cambridge, 1960), 46.

[92] Cf. R. Lattimore in the introduction to his Iliad translation (Chicago, 1965), 43: "as an essential characteristic of the formula is to repeat, an essential of simile is uniqueness." This goes for epic poetry. As W. P. Ker said, *Essays on Medieval Literature* (London, 1905), 41, "the conceits of the courtly poets are handed down like heirlooms from one generation to another." Again, it is not the existence of conventional similes that is striking in Arabic poetry, but their quantity, and that they can be more or less arbitrarily inserted even in good poems. These similes are the arabesques of Goethe's Xenie (*Gedenkausgabe der Werke, Briefe und Gespräche* [Zurich, 1948-1954], II, 514), "Alle die Andern, sie haben zu tragen, zu tun, zu bedeuten. / Wir, das glückliche Volk, brauchen sonst nichts als zu sein."

[93] "It invites things to matter, as things, to man." M. Heidegger, *Unterwegs zur Sprache* (Pfullingen, 1960), 22.

in the effect of a poetic description. Repetition of a word in a specific, restricted context can turn the word into a fetish—witness the vocabulary of literary erotica. Moreover, repetition may also reverse the direction of a simile's or metaphor's effect. The point may be reached where a phrase is associated with poetry as a mode of perception, and its effect will be to transfer the object described into a poetic universe. The image goes from afferent to efferent, from bringing in to carrying out. The word fetish does just this: it pretends to invite a reality to the mind, but in truth it carries the mind out into the shadowy world of its own fabrications.

Repetition escapes this fate only in a poetry that is truly ritualistic, that, like the *qaṣīda*, has a coherent and emotionally valid model of reality to back it up. In the *ḳhamrīyāt*, there are many ritualized actions—the night journey, the opening, mixing and pouring of the wine, etc.—but while these poems have an emotional validity as adjuncts to the model of life and death against which they rebel, in themselves they are a conscious truancy, and their ritualized actions a play. The result of this odd situation is that waists like reeds and faces like moons set off an oscillation—a teetering, one might say—between the body and the body's shadow in the mind.

In this manner, the conventional descriptions in Abū Nuwās remove us into a world that half knows itself to be poetic rather than realistic. The very permanence of images gives this world an air of paradise, a *rêverie hors du monde*, as Massignon said of gardens in Islamic countries.[94] Our garden is already decorated by some of the sapphires and emeralds, by some of the perfumes and other objects of non-nature that run wild in the later poets, but its essential fur-

[94] L. Massignon, "Les méthodes de réalisation artistique de l'islam," *Opera Minora* (Beirut, 1963), III, 16.

nishing is the artificially used language of convention divorced from the purpose of information. For the Chinese poet, *procul negotiis* means drinking his wine in the tranquility of the mountains. For the *khamrīya* poet, turning from the world is turning instead to an ideal agitation of emotion in a world just artificial enough to preclude an intolerable running down of pitch.

6

In the ninth century, a variety of changes occurred in the course of Arabic poetry. Their effects were to be felt for a long time.

An intellectual poetry of *pointes*, of *concordia discors* became fashionable. Some of its aspects are discussed in the next chapter.

At the other end of the scale, a generation or so after Abū Nuwās, poets appeared who, especially in panegyrics, re-established the grand style. They made use of the conventions of the pre-Islamic *qaṣīda*, and delighted in archaic vocabulary as well as in a new rhetorical splendor. Their success forced *ghazal* and *khamrīya* into minor roles, although it must be conceded that the neo-classical style owed much of its vigor to an ability to assimilate touches that the other genres had developed. Chapter v includes a poem of al-Mutanabbī's in which such assimilation is at work.

Ghazal and *khamrīya* acquired symbolic contents and, once more, a profound cultural significance among the mystics: people in whose thinking God and obsession—Islam and poetry—were at peace.

three

Waṣf: Two Views of Time

Of poetic description (*waṣf*) independent of plot or larger framework Ibn al-Muʿtazz (d. 908) was the first major practitioner. His work already contains the salient characteristics of the genre. The chief vehicle of the *waṣf* poem is the simile, less frequently the metaphor. The similes tend to link two prima facie unrelated sets of objects, usually such that the objects within each set stand in some form of coherence. The result is a poetry of wit, with emphasis on astounding combinations. *Waṣf* poems are frequently very short: two or three lines may be the extent of an entire piece.

If the *qaṣīda* experienced time as a medium for various balances; if in the *khamrīya* there was a struggle to hold on to the moment at any cost; the *waṣf* poems I am about to discuss —and they are typical—come after a fork in the road: in one group the speaker eliminates time altogether, and in the other he surrenders to time with his whole being.

1

This is what Ṣanawbarī has to say about the narcissus:

durrun tashaqqaqa ʿan yawāqītin ʿalā
quḍubi z-zumurrudi fawqa busṭi s-sundusi[1]

[1] Ṣanawbarī, *Dīwān*, ed. Iḥsān ʿAbbās (Beirut, 1970), 180-81. Ṣanawbarī died around the middle of the tenth century, but his work

Pearls unfolding from yellow sapphires [which rest] on emerald stems over carpets of fine sundus-silk.

The verse refers a natural object that may elicit esthetic contemplation to an artificial configuration of objects that are considered beautiful in themselves, and whose beauty therefore involves little or no will to art.

Admittedly, the configuration of these objects which are beautiful in themselves is made or imagined by man. It is willed and it is, or might be, made for no other purpose than to give us pleasure. The natural object—the flower—is humanized when it is linked by the simile to such a configuration. Put more precisely: it is enslaved to the esthetic interest.

It is a deceptive humanization, because the comparison between petal and gem is paradoxical. As the flower is turned into a set of esthetic atoms, it ceases to participate in the world of time and process, except by contrast. It is now an alien. To be sure, every man-made esthetic object will be alien in a sense: it will catch a moment or a series of moments and hold them fast. But the combination of objects beautiful in themselves lacks that *aura* of the creative act which retains objects of art within their temporality.[2] Gems seem to radiate their color from within, inexhaustibly. We act upon them to some degree, cut and combine them as we please, but a difference remains between a painter or sculptor and a faceter of precious stones. The one works paint or stone into meaning, the other merely intensifies something that is already in the material. Thus, the artificial flower is not significantly more than the sum of its parts; the *Concert Champêtre* is sig-

---

exemplifies what Ibn al-Mu'tazz (d. A.D. 908) already tends towards in his *waṣf* poems.

[2] The word "aura" is borrowed from Walter Benjamin; cf. *Illuminations*, ed. H. Arendt, transl. H. Zohn (New York, 1969), 221.

nificantly more than the sum of Giorgione's pigments. With the diminution in the esthetic role of the creative act goes a loss of temporality; this loss the poets who embedded gems and other esthetic ultimates in their works considered a gain.

We can now correct our terminology. For a working distinction, let us say that an object that is beautiful in and by itself (or: an object that lies near the beautiful-in-itself end of the scale) is "decorative," while an "esthetic" object is determined by the aura of a will to art. This distinction gets rid of the notion that a decorative object must decorate something, and will permit us to use "decorative," without being derogatory, in speaking of the beautiful-in-itself object that sparkles in the *waṣf*-poem.

The poets of the Middle Ages did not invent out of thin air the changing of natural objects into decorative ultimates. Their world loved decoration: those who could afford it might surround themselves with trees encased in silver, fruits of gold, and pools in which, instead of water, quicksilver reflected the moon.[3] In the medieval observer, gems and precious metals left an impression of admirable atemporality, if for chemical rather than esthetic reasons. In a striking passage of the *Kitāb al-imtāʿ wal-muʾānasa*, Abu Ḥayyān at-Tawḥīdī explains that women and children may be thrilled by novelties, but true dignity belongs to things that are timeless, or, in the temporal realm, to things that are minimally subject to generation, such as gold, sapphires, etc.[4]

Another example will carry us further in our inquiry:

[3] See A. Mez, *Die Renaissance des Islams* (Heidelberg, 1922), 362-63.

[4] Abū Ḥayyān at-Tawḥīdī, *Kitāb al-imtāʿ wal-muʾānasa*, ed. Aḥ. Amīn and Aḥ. az-Zayn (Cairo, 1953), I, 23-24. The idea is just about as old as anything in western literature. Compare the gold and silver dogs that guard Alcinous' house (Odyssey VII, 91-94) and that were made by Hephaestus to be forever immortal and ageless, *hous H. eteuxen . . . athanatous ontas ḳai agērōs ēmata panta.*

wa-ka'anna muḥmarra sh-shaqī-
qi idhā taṣawwaba aw taṣa"ad
a'lāmu yāqūtin nushir-
na 'alā rimāḥin min zabarjad[5]

It is as if the red anemones, as they sway up and down, / were banners of red sapphire upon chrysolite spears.

The second line stiffens the movement described by the first. We know that chrysolite spears, whatever their effect in a museum, will not be much good on the battlefield, and we note with some perplexity that sapphire banners will lack the essential quality of flapping in the wind. The esthetic reduction is twofold: the flower is compared to a flag that is already reduced to its sapphire-and-chrysolite double. All of which is rather strange when we consider that we are hearing about anemones in motion. Even a machine—and medieval people thought sleight-of-hand machinery great fun—could not copy the free variations in the movement of a windblown flower or flag.

In the *Arabian Nights*, the depths that hide gadgets of supernatural power contain such tussauderies of gold and precious stones. Objects without temporality, and Aladdin's tarnished old lamp—object fallen into desuetude, fallen out of time—together furnish the magic cellar.

Indeed, there is a magical aspect to the entire operation we are witnessing. The mood of *ḳenosis* that in various guises survived in *ghazal* and *ḳhamrīya* is now gone. The self has retreated; the speaker would keep the poet's give-and-take with the world but without hazarding an emotional investment in the temporal.

I will clarify what I mean by this give-and-take. There is a curious notion, and one that has been passed down in our

[5] Ṣanawbarī, *Dīwān*, 477.

schools, one may assume, since time immemorial, that a simile serves to clarify something and to render it more vivid by means of a sort of explanation. In nearly every case, this notion is nonsense. That it is nonsense is hardly a discovery. The Russian critic V. Shklovsky, for example, reminds his readers of Gogol's comparison of the sky with the clothes of God:[6] an association with more power than analytic clarity in it. And we should not for a moment suppose that the simile that more or less obscures the simple object occurs only in modern literature. M. Nuwayhī has discussed an example in detail: 'Alqama's comparison of a wine-jug with a gazelle standing on a hilltop (*Mufaḍḍalīyāt*, 120:44).[7] Nor does the visually precise simile necessarily yield more explanation than opacity, an impression of things unplumbed: corpses with skin swollen like the bark of the tragacanth after rain (*Muf.* 53:7); foliage waving in the wind like girls pulling at one another's hair (*Muf.* 14:7), and so on. Shklovsky has argued that art means to snap us out of our habits of perception, to increase the difficulty and length of perception, because the process of perception is an esthetic end in itself.[8] It seems to me that another step must still be taken: the job of a simile, of this autocratic setting up of relations in the world, is to turn the world into a code with an uncertain meaning.

That objects combine into chords makes the world more profound, more musical. By making a simile, we produce a clue that in turn generates a puzzle. We have this satisfaction in exchange, that the terms of comparison meet in our minds to spark their intrigue and their mystery.

A simile must be more than the sum of its parts, because it is only the entrance to the labyrinth of its immanent possibil-

[6] See *Russian Formalist Criticism*, ed. and transl. L. T. Lemon and M. J. Reis (Lincoln, Nebraska, 1965), 6.

[7] *ash-Shi'r al-jāhilī*, I, 107-20.

[8] *Russian Formalist Criticism*, 12.

ities. Ṣanawbarī's flower is one of the rare instances where comparison really causes reduction rather than complexity. The objects to which the flower is compared are decorative atoms: they define a single track—the decorative—for the simile, and we would be looking in vain for great skeins of meaning—unless we were looking at the motives for the act of reduction itself.

The poet loses the mystery of the simile by using objects that he has chosen for their immunity to time. Out with the mystery goes our experience of having contributed to the world by combining its notes into music: the decorative atoms fit into no chord, gain nothing by the simile, and remain self-sufficient. By enslaving the world to the decorative, we have lost communion with it.

Of all these things, the poem from which my first quote comes speaks most eloquently:

1 a-ra'ayta aḥsana min 'uyūni n-narjisi
am min talāḥuẓihinna wasṭa l-majlisi
2 durrun tashaqqaqa 'an yawāqītin 'alā
quḍubi z-zumurrudi fawqa busṭi s-sundusi
3 ajfānu kāfūrin khafaqna bi-a'yunin
min za'farānin nā'imāti l-malmasi

Have you seen anything prettier than the eyes of jonquils, or the glances they cast at one another in the midst of a party? / Pearls unfolding from yellow sapphires that rest on emerald stems over carpets of fine sundus-silk. / Eyelids of camphor that flutter in saffron eyes, delicate to the touch.

In these first three lines, once again we have a twofold reduction, but it is somewhat different from the previous one (see page 81). The eye-metaphor on which the first line is built is immediately dismantled in the second, and the flower as flower is translated into precious stones. In the third line the metaphor is recovered, but now the eyes are no longer linked to the flower, but to colorful herbs—another essential decorative element of the period.[9] In other words, the metaphor from nature in line one has been broken into two sets of metaphors, both aiming at decorative ultimates: gems and herbs. The next line is another sideways step:

4 wa-ka'annahā aqmāru laylin aḥdaqat
bi-shumūsi dajnin fawqa ghuṣnin amlasi

It is as if night-time moons encircled suns in the dark over smooth branches.

The eye is abandoned here, and the flower is given a new part-by-part metamorphosis. After terms of comparison that had duration but no history, we now get a combination that cannot possibly exist outside the poet's fancy. Objective, measurable time is blocked in this verse, which works night and day into a single moment.

In the next line,

5 mughrawriqātun fī taraqruqi ṭallihā
tarnū runūwa n-nāẓiri l-mutafarrisi

They are drowned in tears, with the glitter of dew upon them; they stare with a scrutinizing eye.

there is a return to the beginning, at least in the sense that once again we have both the eye and the flower. The image

[9] Cf. Abū 'Alī l-Muḥassin at-Tanūkhi, *Kitāb jamī' at-tawārikh* (*al-musammā bi-nishwār al-muḥāḍara wa-akhbār al-mudhākara*), ed. D. S. Margoliouth (London, 1921), 144-45, an anecdote about the caliph ar-Rāḍi.

is somewhat peculiar: we do not quite know what to make of the combination of tearful eyes and staring eyes. It is at best less than emotionally straight, and perhaps it is absurd to common sense. But, as it happens, the "staring" is picked up at the end of the poem, and it figures in the main line of thought.

Verse six brings one more reduction of the kind we have been discussing:

6 fa-idhā taghashshathā r-riyāḥu tanaffasat
'an mithli rīḥi l-miski ayya tanaffusi

And when the winds strike them, they exhale something like the fragrance of musk. What a breath!

By now, the flower has been transmuted into all three of the decorative elements that, on the basis of medieval texts, we would expect to see: gems, aromatic herbs, perfumes. Not every reduction succeeds in taking every component of the flower into account; indeed, the last one deals with a single newly introduced characteristic, but this does not affect the bouquet of the whole. After the last variation, there is a sudden return to the human analogy proposed in the first line, and the description is allowed an emotional overtone:

7 wa-ḥakā tadānī ba'ḍihā min ba'ḍihā
yawman tadāniya mu'nisin min mu'nisi

Their closeness to one another resembles the closeness, one day, of friend to friend.

We are reminded of *talāḥuẓ*, "casting glances at each other," in the opening verse. As in line four, the initial conjunction between flower and eye is revived. It is in addition given an emotional direction; one might say it is saved from neutrality. The mood lasts through the next line, a very bad one, which explains that people embrace at parties and flowers in flowerbeds. Then it collapses:

9 wa-idhā naʻasta mina l-mudāmi ra'aytahā
tarnū ilayka bi-aʻyunin lam tanʻasi

And if you grow drowsy with wine you see them staring at you with undrowsy eyes.

Formally the conjunction is still there. In contents it is broken. It is remarkable how the opposition between the two half-lines is set off by the metrical scheme. The meter is *kāmil*, trimeter acatalectic, in which the half-line is constituted by three feet of the form – – ⏑ – or ⏑ ⏑ – ⏑ –. 9a is the fastest of all the half-lines in the poem (it is the only one in which all three feet begin with an anapest rather than a sponde), but 9b puts on the brakes, using – – ⏑ – twice and ⏑ ⏑ – ⏑ – only once.

"You see them staring" takes us directly back to line four, and now the peculiarity of the tear-drowned but scrutinizing eyes becomes a little more understandable. It is not at all resolved; rather, the contradiction that is only sensed in line four is now explicitly revealed. A structural see-sawing that goes on throughout the poem at last becomes part of the contents. There has been a vacillation between comparison with the fixed or fantastic on the one hand, and with the natural and mutable on the other. To the latter, the more or less untranslatable *yawman*, "one day," in line seven—conventional *metri causa* padding though it is—gives the required flavor of temporality. But you cannot very well have it both ways. As your eyes begin to close, the flower's eye continues its scrutiny of you. It is not a friend after all: it is not a *you* but an *it*—Ṣanawbarī's poem puts into words the esthetic implications of the genre to which it belongs.

There are three more lines. In these the motif of the glance finds its rightful owner: the saki who holds the poet's life in his hands. The last line,

awqa'ta qalbī bayna laḥẓin muṭmi'in
fī l-wuddi minka wa-bayna lafẓin mu'yisi

Joining to glances that make me yearn for your love
words that bring despair, you have prostrated my heart.

beats a retreat to a frustrated desire that is less uncomfortable than enduring the gaze that the enchanted flower fixes upon the sorcerer.

2

In the second group of poems, time, far from being denied, haunts the very structure of composition.

a-mā tarā n-narjisa l-mayyāsa yalḥaẓunā
alḥāẓa dhī faraḥin bil-'atbi masrūri
ka'anna aḥdāqahā fī ḥusni ṣūratihā
madāhinu t-tibri fī awrāqi kāfūri
ka'anna ṭalla n-nadā fīhī li-mubṣirihī
dam'un taraqraqa min ajfāni mahjūri[10]

Do you not see the swaggering narcissus casting at us the glances of a joyous person [i.e. a Cruel Beauty] delighted by a lover's reproaches? / In the beauty of their form,

[10] Ibn al-Mu'tazz, *Dīwān*, ed. Muḥyiddīn al-Khayyāṭ (Damascus, 1951), 317. Not included in the partial edition of his *Dīwān* by B. Lewin (Istanbul, 1945-1950).

> *the pupils of their eyes resemble golden unguent boxes amid leaves of camphor. / To the beholder, the dew upon the narcissus resembles tears that glitter from the eyelids of a forsaken lover.*

In many ways, this flower is a great deal like Ṣanawbarī's. The purpose to which the conventional images are put is quite different.

The first and third verses go together; the middle verse seems extraneous to the logical progression of the poem. In lines one and three, we have on the left side (of transcription and translation, that is) two states of one object (narcissus without and with dew) and on the right one asymmetrical relation with two contrasting functions (cruel beloved: happy —shunned lover: glum). But the truth of the matter is that we are shown not two successive states of the flower but simply two glimpses of it, in such a way that the second time around we notice the dewdrops we had missed at first. Especially because the segments on the right-hand side are contrasted, a peculiar time-lag is felt. In Ṣanawbarī's lines about anemones (p. 81) the windblown flowers were reduced to immobility and thus deprived of perceptible time. In turn, the narcissus is observed piecemeal, in discrete segments of time. What we get from the poet is not the unfolding of possible analogies to one object, nor a continuous sweep of the eye, but a double-take. The interruption by the second verse—assuming that it is in its correct place—emphasizes the discreteness of the two observations.

The sense of a double-take creates a certain imbalance between the two sides of the comparisons in lines one and three. The following chart represents this imbalance, *L* and *R* standing for the left and right sides of transliteration and translation:

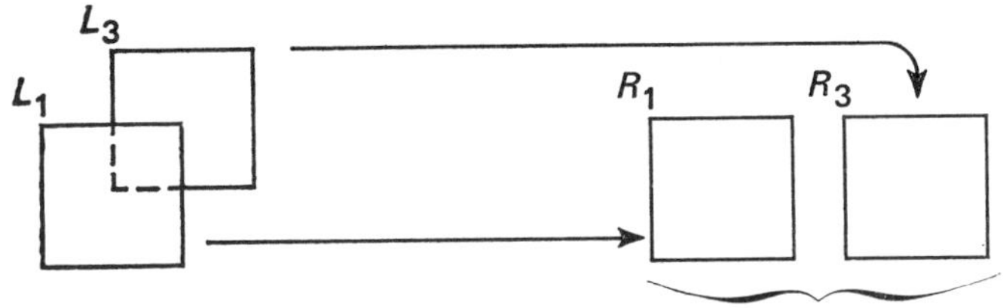

L_3 is placed behind L_1, being a perception of the same object. R_1 and R_3 are separate, although they may be bracketed as functions of a single relation. Subliminally desiring to correct the imbalance—a desire of the mind, which it is perhaps the chief merit of historical linguistics to have demonstrated—the reader will do one of two things. He may resolve that in reality we are seeing two different flowers, and consequently pull out L_3 from behind L_1. Or else he may accede to the insinuation of a now-you-see-it-now-you-don't character in the other side, the bracketed R_1 and R_3. The first solution is rather the less gripping of the two. If the reader chooses to come to an equilibrium by allowing R_3 to overlap R_1, the poem will say that causing pain and suffering pain may abruptly follow each other in the same person; and then, if L_1 and L_3 imply that perception is experienced in discrete segments of time, R_1 and R_3 imply that emotions too come in discrete segments: that successive emotions in the same person are not only fugitive but also fragmentary, and—being experienced as non-contiguous—unaccountable.

Although it was possible to assign verse two a role within the poem, there is no escaping the truth that it pulls the other way: towards duration without history. By contrast, in Ṣanawbarī a centrifugal pull came from the obvious temporality of the word *yawman*, "one day." As in many poems of this period, a pendulum swings between two poles: experiencing time by making the sense of its discreteness into a principle of poetic structure, and rejecting the experience altogether. In our last example, decorative reduction as a mode of pure duration appeared for a moment in line two as a tempting luxury, if also as an explicatory contrast.

It is quite conceivable that this type of *waṣf* poem was led to its attitude towards time by a basic technique for setting up intriguing conceits. The trick is to take two objects or qualities A_1 and B_1 that harmoniously coexist in a set S_1, and then metaphorically translate them into objects or qualities A_2 and B_2 that belong to a single set S_2, but that are in some sense contraries. Compare the following verse:

wa-suhaylun ka-wajnati l-ḥibbi fī l-law-
ni wa-qalbi l-muḥibbi fī l-khafaqāni[11]

While Canopus resembles in color the cheek of the beloved, and in throbbing the heart of the lover . . .

Color and throbbing are simply concomitant in S_1 (the star), while the cheek of the beloved and the heart of the lover show two complementary modes of excitement in S_2. For another example, here is a Hebrew couplet by Moshe Ibn Ezra, in which the same technique is used:

vᵉ-tappūᵃḥ emet ēl lō bᵉrā'ō
lᵉbad 'ōneg lᵉmerīᵃḥ vᵉnōshēq
ḥᵃshabtīhū bᵉ-shūr yārōq vᵉ-ādōm
qᵉbuṣīm bō pᵉnēy ḥāshūq vᵉ-ḥōshēq[12]

In truth, God did not create apples merely as a delectation for those who smell them or leave in them the mark

[11] I have been unable to locate this verse in the works of Abū l-'Alā l-Ma'arrī, to whom it is attributed by M. M. 'Abdalḥamīd in his *Sharḥ maqāmāt Badī' az-Zamān al-Hamadhānī*, 419.

[12] See H. Shirman (ed)., *ha-Shira ha-'ibrit bi-Sfarad u-bi-Provans* (Jerusalem and Tel Aviv, 1961), I, 374.

of their teeth! / As I observe an apple in which red and green are joined, I think I see the faces of lover and beloved.

The lover is sick with desire, the beloved blushes, and a very pretty relation obtains between S_1 and S_2. This is a favorite combinatory method, and the next poem, by Ibn al-Mu'tazz, demonstrates how easily the contrasting terms of one set can form a temporal sequence:

kam qad qaṭa'tu ilayka min daymūmatin
nuṭafu l-miyāhi bihā sawādu n-nāẓiri
fī laylatin fīhā s-samā'u mulimmatun
sawdā'u muẓlimatun ka-qalbi l-kāfiri
wal-barqu yakhṭifu min khilāli saḥābihā
khaṭfa l-fu'ādi li-maw'idin min zā'iri
wal-ghaythu munhallun yasuḥḥu ka'annahū
dam'u l-muwaddi'i ithra ilfin sā'iri[13]

How many deserts have I crossed on my way to you! Deserts in which all the drops of water together were no bigger than the pupil of the eye![14] / During a night when clouds hung low in the sky, and the sky was pitch black like an unbeliever's heart, / while lightning would be flashing from chinks in the clouds as the heart flashes at the time appointed for a visitor, / and while the rain-clouds poured down torrents like the tears of one who

[13] Ibn al-Mu'tazz, *Dīwān*, 318.

[14] Perhaps Ibn al-Mu'tazz means "the only drops of water were [of] the pupil of the eye," i.e., either the humor of vision (cf., for example, *The Book of the Ten Treatises on the Eye Ascribed to Hunain Ibn Is-haq*, Arabic text ed. and transl. M. Meyerhof [Cairo, 1928], p. 73 of the Arabic and p. 3 of the English text) or the aqueous element in the eye, discussed by Aristotle, *De anima*, III/1, 425a, of which the poet could have read the translation by Ḥunayn's son, Isḥāq.

is saying goodbye as he follows a friend departing in the night.

There are three principal contrasts in the poem. First, the second half brings flashes of light and a downpour to balance the darkness and the arid landscape in the first. This contrast is put chiastically. Second, the comparisons go from static to dramatic. Third, built into the similes of the second half is the contrast the poem is really after: arrival and departure. The other contrasts simply orchestrate this last one.

The technique I have described comes into play in lines three and four, where various simultaneous events are related by circumstantial clauses, but where simultaneity is dissected by the similes into a temporal sequence: lightning goes with arrival, rain with the tears of parting. As in the previous examples, A_1 and B_1 normally coexist while A_2 and B_2 make up an opposition, but now the opposition quite naturally suggests a passage of time. The reader will note that the desert too has two states: the first and fourth lines cannot be describing simultaneous events. Everything is open to sudden change, to time in which one discrete segment follows another.

My last exhibit comes from Hebrew poetry, but it is obviously of the genre we are discussing and rooted in the Arabic tradition. The poem is by Samuel ha-Nagid:[15]

1 aṣappe elēy shaḥaq v^e-kokābāv
v^e-abbīṭ b^e-ereṣ et r^emāśeyhā

[15] See *ha-Shira ha-ʿibrit,* I, 136. Shirman presents the text of the poem as it appears in Samuel ha-Nagid's *Ben Qohelet.* This is the text I cite. The poet incorporated it into a longer poem in another book of his, cf. *Divan Sh^emu'el ha-Nagid (Ben T^ehillim),* ed. D. Yarden (Jerusalem, 1966), 151-52.

2 v^{e}-ābīn b^{e}-libbī kī y^{e}ṣīrātām
y^{e}ṣīrā m^{e}ḥukkāmā b^{e}-ma'śeyhā
3 r^{e}'ū et sh^{e}mēy mārōm k^{e}mō qubbā
t^{e}fūrīm b^{e}-lūlā'ōt q^{e}rāseyhā
4 v^{e}-sahar v^{e}-kokābāv k^{e}mō rō'ā
t^{e}shallaḥ b^{e}-tōk āḥū k^{e}bāśeyhā
5 k^{e}-illū l^{e}bānā bēyn n^{e}śī'ēy 'āb
s^{e}fīnā m^{e}halleket b^{e}-nisseyhā
6 v^{e}-'ānān k^{e}-'almā al p^{e}nēy ginnā
t^{e}hallēk v^{e}-tashqe et hadasseyhā
7 v^{e}-'āb ṭal k^{e}mō na'rā t^{e}na'ēr min
ś^{e}'ārāh 'alēy ereṣ r^{e}sīseyhā
8 v^{e}-shōknīm k^{e}mō ḥayyā asher nāṭ^{e}tā
l^{e}-līnā v^{e}-ḥaṣrōtām abūseyhā
9 v^{e}-kullām y^{e}nūsūn mē-ḥatat māvet
k^{e}-yōnā asher han-nēṣ y^{e}nīsehā
10 v^{e}-sōfām l^{e}-hiddammōt l^{e}-ṣallaḥat
asher shibb^{e}rū kātīt ḥarāśeyhā

1 I observe the sky and its stars, and glance at the earth and the things that creep upon it.
2 I realize that their creation was wisely carried out.
3 Look at the heavens high up: they are like a domed tent, the loops along the flaps being clasped together by hooks.
4 The moon and the stars that go with it are like a shepherdess who sends her lambs to the water meadow.
5 Among scudding clouds, the moon seems a ship moving under its banners.
6 The cloud is like a young woman walking in a garden, watering her myrtles.
7 The cloudy haze of dew is like a girl shaking out upon the earth the drops of water from her hair.
8 And the inhabitants are like a beast that lies down to sleep; their enclosed courts are the stables.

9 *All of them flee from the terror of death, as a dove that the hawk pursues.*
10 *And their end is to be compared with a plate that someone has smashed into sherds.*

The poem naturally falls into three parts. The first two lines are prefatory; the last two form a conclusion. The longest section, lines 3-7, consists in a set of comparisons, in each of which term *A* is a celestial or atmospheric object, and term *B* a terrestrial object of some kind. Series *A* is constructed in such a way as to give the impression of a connected sequence: sky—moon and stars—moon among clouds—cloud—cloudy haze of dew. There is a clear downward motion from "heavens up high" to "haze of dew." The experience is obviously spatial, brought about by a broad downward sweep of the eye, although the line followed is not absolutely continuous. A cascade effect is caused when components of series *A* appear in a certain verse and then reappear, in a different visual syntagm, in the next: "moon among stars"—"moon among clouds," etc. On the plane of vocabulary, a synonymic variation (*sahar* and *l^ebānā* for "moon," *'ānān* and *'āb* for "cloud") parallels the sense of seeing the same object in a new light. A jerkiness results that recalls the views of the narcissus or the desert storm in Ibn al-Mu'tazz. Before I discuss its effect on the poem as a whole, I must turn to series *B*, the right-hand side of the comparisons.

Unlike its counterpart, series *B* consists of terms that are not motivated by one another but only by their successive analogues on the left. The curious thing about the terms of series *B* is their similarity to one another. Three of the five involve a woman and water, and water occurs in yet a fourth (verse 5). The structural contrast between the two series reflects a fundamental principle of language itself.

The similar images of series *B* correspond to a substitution set in the vocabulary, that is to say to a group of semantically kindred words only one of which will be picked by the speaker for a given slot in an utterance. This manner of grouping words (e.g., "forest/wood/copse") represents one axis of the semiological code; the other axis has to do with the way in which one element may follow another in an actual syntagm (e.g., "moth-eaten dragon" may occur, "moth-eat dragon" may not). As Saussure puts it, a substitution set exists *in absentia* (i.e., in the speaker's mind) and is a virtual mnemonic series, while a set of words forming an actual syntagm exists *in praesentia*.[16]

Now the objects that form series *A* in our poem are in a relation of visual contiguity, and they clearly correspond in visual terms to a set of elements arranged *in praesentia*. The objects of series *B* strike one as a substitution set (all but one of whose constituents ought to be *in absentia*), but that has not undergone the selection process usual in speech. The *contrast* between the two semiological axes brings memory into play—Saussure's phrase is no metaphor.

"Shepherdess, girl, young woman"—the series that should exist only mnemonically, *in absentia*—balances moon, stars, and the rest, as though the depth of remembrance were being scoured to help the onlooker breathe under the vast spaces described in series *A*. He seizes on memory, not so much any specific content of it as the free movement through time to which memory pretends—the echoes through time in Ner-

[16] F. de Saussure, *Cours de linguistique générale*, ed. C. Bally and A. Schehaye (Paris, 1962), 170-71. To R. Jakobson belongs the merit of having first recognized how important a role Saussure's distinction can play in stylistic analysis; cf. "Two Aspects of Language and Two Types of Aphasic Disturbances," in R. Jakobson and M. Halle, *Fundamentals of Language* ('s-Gravenhage, 1956), 55-82.

val's *Sylvie*, the taste of the *madeleine*. The specific image ("woman" + "water") does, nonetheless, promote the desired effect: emotively, because its gentle figures offer a contrast to the grander objects of the night sky, and structurally, because "woman" + "water" is a literary archetype in the Near East. The combination of the words *ṭal* and *r^esiseyhā* sends the audience directly back to Song of Songs 5:2,[17] but we may also think of our first glimpses of Rebecca, Gen. 24:11-15, and of Rachel, Gen. 29:8-10.[18] That the poet's contemporaries, reared on textual exegesis, would have instinctively analyzed the "woman" + "water" images into their components and then into the underlying archetype, I have no doubt.

Very subtly, the audience has been made to sense that memory provides the mind with an inner space and a freedom from the here-and-now, but in line eight these notions are given a wrench, and in the final couplet they are denied. In line eight, the path followed by series *A* comes down to earth, and at once the substitution set on the right-hand side is broken off. "The inhabitants" are a class of which the class "shepherdess/girl/young woman" properly forms a part, so that we have a shift of the class "human beings" from one side of the word *ḳ^emō*, "like," to the other. This is a formal switch signaling that we are moving from class to class in a broader sense than had been apparent in the middle section of the poem. More is being presented than a single set of analogues to meteorological matters. We are confronted with a set of sets arranged in descending order: celestial objects and atmospheric phenomena—human beings—beasts and birds—

[17] Shirman, *loc.cit.*

[18] Compare the meeting between Enkidu and the temple prostitute in *Gilgamesh*, tablet 1, col. 4. Also comparable is, I think, the meeting with the Laestrygonian princess at the Artacian spring (Od. x, 105-08).

clay. The descending line observed in the spatial arrangement and in this classification is paralleled in the grammar of the concluding verses, with the verbs moving away from the active mode. In the middle section, the human beings in series *B* are subjects with active-transitive verbs. In line seven, the connection between subject and active verb is even pantomimed by paronomasia: *naʿrā/tᵉnaʿēr*. In the switch-line immediately following, the verb is no longer transitive, and it is no longer assigned to the human beings in the line, but to the next class down: "the inhabitants [are] like a beast that lies down to sleep." (In Hebrew, the copula has a zero form in the present tense.) In line nine, term *B* of the comparison has no verb at all; instead, it is the antecedent of a relative clause of which it turns out to be the object: "as a dove that the hawk pursues." Once again, there is an assonance linking "flee," "dove," and "pursue," but now the action that is acoustically linked to the object of comparison is endured rather than performed by that object. In this verse there is still a named outside agent—the hawk. In the concluding line, the last term *B* is the object (via a relative clause again) of a crushingly impersonal verb: "a plate that someone has smashed."

The mood created by the spatial downward line—down to the potsherds falling to the ground—is not unaffected by the descending order of categories from heaven to clay and by the sequence of verb forms. To follow it through is *sentir l'horrible fardeau du Temps qui brise vos épaules et vous penche vers la terre.*[19] The jerkiness we noticed in the spatial sequence gains a meaning when, in the last two verses, memory is checkmated. The single sweep of the eye was analyzed into segments: the world-scape that expands over us in a tranquil vastness could be grasped only part by part; it was

[19] Baudelaire, *Oeuvres complètes*, ed. Y.-G. Le Dantec and C. Pichois (Paris, 1961), 286. (*Le spleen de Paris*, XXXIII.)

perceived by retakes. The cascade effect was not only spatial but also temporal: the divisibility of the sweeping glance is also witness to the arbitrary shears of time.

At last the code invades the contents: *sōfām l^{e}-hiddammōt,* "their end is to be compared." Perhaps this impingement is more than a poetic mannerism; perhaps it goes some of the way toward redeeming the experience of memory. Their end is to be compared; we do the comparing. We are imprisoned in time, every bit as much as the things that surround us; to compare, to sort out the relations about us, to actively experience our being in time is making the best of it.

Technique

four

The Poem and its Parts

TIME and again Western scholars suggest that it is no use looking for coherence in a medieval Arabic poem, and we have even managed to persuade many of our Middle Eastern colleagues that those of their poets who were unlucky enough to be born before 1930 never composed anything but a crazy-quilt of glittering lines. But things are, for once, a little better than they seem. I will try to demonstrate by a few examples, mostly taken from Abū Nuwās, that some medieval poems really hang together quite well. The discussion is in two sections: the first deals with poems whose coherence rests upon the use of elementary rhetorical devices, and the second examines a few methods of transition and conclusion.

1

The following short poem is characterized by intricate formal play based on antitheton, the use of contrasting words.

sa-uʿṭīki r-riḍā wa-amūtu ghamman
wa-askutu lā ughimmuki bil-ʿitābi
ʿahidtuki marratan tanwīna waṣlī
wa-anti l-yawma tahwayna jtinābī
wa-ghayyaraki z-zamānu wa-kullu shay'in
yaṣīru ilā t-taghayyuri wadh-dhahābi
fa-in kāna ṣ-ṣawābu ladayki hajrī
fa-ʿammāki l-ilāhu ʿani ṣ-ṣawābi[1]

[1] *Dīwān Abī Nuwās*, 56. Translated in Wagner, *Abū Nuwās*, 316. In

I will make you content and die of grief. I will be silent, not grieving you with reproaches. / I knew you once when you wanted to be with me, but today you desire to avoid me. / Time has changed you, but then, everything tends towards change and passing away. / But, if in your opinion the right course of action is to break up with me, may God blind you to the right course.

The first line, based on a clear contrast although not on a precise antitheton, deals with the motif of the lover's willingness to suffer at the hands of the beloved. The second line gives us a kind of backdrop to this, in highly structured form, relying on both antitheton and the use of parallel syntax in the two half lines. This much is simple enough, but the line contains subtle shadings of the basic contrast. First: in the Arabic there is a morphological agreement between the two present-tense verbs *tanwīna*, "you want," and *tahwayna*, "you desire," but the agreement is deceptive because in the sentence only *tahwayna* functions as a present, while *tanwīna* forms a circumstantial clause to a past action. The grammatical sleight of hand by which the isocolon is achieved reinforces the contrast between present and remembered past. Second: the associations in the two verbs for "want" and "desire" substantiate the opposition between present and past. If *tahwayna* brings to mind *hawā*, "passion,"—which exists now only in recollection—the verb *tanwīna* is revealed to have been ominous when the reader gets to *ijtinābī*, "to avoid me." At that moment a second meaning of the verb *nawā* begins to haunt the first, namely "to depart." The verb, with the latter meaning, is common in the *nasīb* tradition.[2] The elegant

the Beirut 1965 edition of his poems, this quatrain is attributed to al-'Abbās ibn al-Aḥnaf.

[2] There is in fact a tradition of using *hawā* and *nawā* close together,

play of parallels and contrasts becomes, by way of these associations, a linguistic reflection of recalling the past, and a linguistic insinuation of the immanence in the past of the present.

What was insinuation in the second line becomes explicit theory in the third. The greater part of that line consists in a statement of a general rule, a *gnōmē*—a figure common in Arabic poetry from the earliest period on.[3] The rule "everything tends towards change" weights the main statement "time has changed you" with the predictability of occurrence that common sense likes to ascribe to the workings of a natural law. But the rule takes in more than the change it documents: besides "change," it includes "passing away." Consequently we have an incomplete proportion in the line, of the following form: "You have changed" : "All things change" $= x$: "All things pass out of existence." Mortality is introduced by subterfuge, by a logical gap. We would wish to apply "passing away" to the emotions in question, but the grammar forces us back to the proportion waiting to be solved, and to the pronoun "you." At first we may think that we have been simply tricked into a pleasurable melancholy, but in the last line the poet makes use of this parallel between the transience of man and his emotions: he knocks his head against it. This last line contains no formal antitheton, but it is contrary to the basic statement in line one (in fact it takes back the promise that was made there) and it is paradoxical that it comes right after the theory expressed in line three. "May God blind you

to denote love and separation. Cf. Majnūn Laylā, *Dīwān*, ed. 'Abdassattār Farrāj (Cairo, no date), nos. 101 and 144.

[3] In our poem built on contrasts and contradictions, it will add to our reading of the third line if we think of the *gnōmē* as it is described in the *Kitāb naqd ash-shi'r*: as a means to eliminate doubts or contradictions. Cf. *The Kitāb naqd al-ši'r of Qudāma b. Ǧa'far al-Kātib al-Baġdādī*, ed. S. A. Bonebakker (Leiden, 1956), 81.

to the right course"—the line contains its own paradox. In these ways, the last line does form a kind of antitheton that extends over the entire quatrain.

If the third line gives premonitions of resignation, the fourth surprises us by reaching out after the straw of paradox. So the poem leaves us not with the poise of resignation or of true hope, but with a self-contradiction. Carrying out the proposal of the first line is certainly no longer possible. We see now that polarity is not an accidental decorative device, a mere *schema lexeos*, but the basic schema for the grasping of emotions in the poem.[4]

A charming description of a bathing woman has been ascribed both to Abū Nuwās and to Ibn al-Mu'tazz.[5] Judging by its style, Ibn al-Mu'tazz is the more likely author. I adduce it here as a particularly straightforward and good example

[4] The extent to which unresolved polarity forms part of the conceptual framework in the poem is shown by a comparison with a poem which is similar in many ways: Pushkin's "I have loved you . . ." (*Ya vas lyubil . . .* , *The Oxford Book of Russian Verse* [Oxford, 1948], 60). Pushkin's poem too deals with love that is nominally given up. It moves from a last bit of hope in the will-o'-the-wisp of the enjambment at the end of the first line ("I have loved you. Love perhaps still / has not been completely extinguished in my soul") on to the main statement in line three, which parallels the opening line in *sa-u'ṭīki r-riḍā*: "But may it no longer trouble you, / I do not want to cause you grief in any way." Finally, after a description of the passions of the past, the poem arrives at an equilibrium, a prayer of resignation and charity: "I loved you so sincerely, so tenderly / as may God grant that you should be loved by another." The Abū Nuwās poem prefers the inharmonics: it moves from the poise of resignation towards the will-o'-the-wisp.

[5] *Dīwān Abī Nuwās*, 27; L. Cheikho-F. E. Bustānī, *al-Majānī l-ḥadītha* (Beirut, 1961), III, 60. Not in the Cairo 1953 edition of Abū Nuwās by Ghazzālī. Ascribed to Ibn al-Mu'tazz in Ibshīhī, *al-Mustaṭraf* (Būlāq, 1869), II, 23, but not in his *Dīwān* (Damascus, 1951) nor among the poems edited by Lewin (Istanbul, 1945-1950). The version above is from the *Mustaṭraf*, but in lines 1-6 the variations are minimal.

of a poem where rhetorical patterns go hand in hand with the perception of reality. The poem uses parallelisms and contrasts, moving from the tranquil idyll of the bathing woman to a disruption caused by a surreptitious observer. She notices him in line five; until then the poet steers his course by a series of parallels:

(1) naḍat ʻanhā l-qamīṣa li-ṣabbi mā'i
fa-warrada khaddahā farṭu l-ḥayā'i
(2) wa-qābalati l-hawā'a wa-qad taʻarrat
bi-muʻtadilin araqqa mina l-hawā'i
(3) wa-maddat rāḥatan kal-mā'i minhā
ilā mā'in ʻatīdin fī inā'i[6]

She stripped off her shift to pour the water, and excessive modesty made her cheeks red. / Naked, she presented to the air a finely proportioned body more delicate than air, / and stretched out a palm like water to water made ready in a jug.

In the fifth line, where the harmony is disturbed, there is a turn to antitheton:

(5) ra'at shakhṣa r-raqībi ʻalā tadānin
fa-asbalati ẓ-ẓalāma ʻalā ḍ-ḍiyā'i
(6a) fa-ghāba ṣ-ṣubḥu minhā taḥta laylin

She saw the approaching figure of the spy, and she let down darkness [her hair] over the light, / so that her morning vanished under night ...

Now we return to parallelism:

[6] The rhetoric recalls the description of a bather by Rufinus, *Greek Anthology* V:60, especially the phrase *hudatos hugroterō khrōti*, "with flesh more fluid than water."

(6b) wa-ẓalla l-māʾu yaqṭiru fawqa māʾi

... and water [tears] kept falling in drops over water,

and the result, prepared by the rhetorical structure so far, is an emotional return to harmony, to a new harmony of bather and water. Cheikho-Bustānī and the Beirut *Dīwān* add one more line here, whose only remaining function is to frame the picture by a switch from description to direct statement:

(7) fa-subḥāna l-ilāhi wa-qad barāhā
ka-aḥsani mā yakūnu mina n-nisāʾi

Glory to God, for he made her the most beautiful of women!

2

Abū Nuwās often pays close attention to the pleasing and proportionate setting out of his matter, and he uses a number of conventional signposts to alert the audience to the nature of his plan. The most common transition marker in his work is inherited from the pre-Islamic age. It is the *waw-rubba* construction, *wa-* followed by a noun in the genitive case. The phrase introduced by *wa-* is very often a conventional one, so that the reader will at once know what to expect. The traditional translation of the *waw rubba* is "many a . . . ," which can be quite misleading. M. J. de Goeje pointed out that frequently there is no idea of plurality involved at all, and he suggested as translations of the non-pluralizing *waw rubba* such phrases as "I remember a . . ." or "O, that . . . ," etc.,[7] which merely indicate that a new topic is being introduced. At times, it seems to me, the function of the *waw rubba* be-

[7] W. Wright, *A Grammar of the Arabic Language*, 3rd ed. (Cambridge, 1964), II, 217.

fore a singular noun is to fudge the difference between singular and plural, and slyly to blur the line between *topos* and event. When the plurality of the thing described is to be made explicit, a plural noun may follow the *wa-*.[8]

Let us now examine the use of *waw rubba* as a transition marker in two texts. In the first, transition is gradual, in the second abrupt. The poem that begins with the famous line,

a-lā fa-sqinī khamran wa-qul lī hiya l-khamru
wa-lā tasqinī sirran idhā amkana l-jahru[9]

Pour me wine and tell me it is wine. Do not pour for me in secret if doing it in the open is possible,

consists of two parts, more or less equal in length. The first half (vss. 1-6) is built upon abstract statements that are a kind of argumentative support for the first line, making a case for drinking:

(2a) fa-'ayshu l-fatā fī sakratin ba'da sakratin . . .

The life of a proper young fellow consists in drunkenness after drunkenness . . .

[8] Cf. *wa-fityatin ḳa-maṣābīḥi d-dujā ghurarin* . . . , "Companions, shining as lanterns in the gloom . . . ," *Dīwān Abī Nuwās*, 111.

[9] *Dīwān Abī Nuwās*, 242; *Diwan des Abu nowas*, ed. Ahlwardt (Greifswald, 1861), no. 29. In Ahlwardt and in the Cairo 1953 ed. by Ghazzālī, two lines are missing that are included in the Cairo 1898 ed. of the *dīwān* by M. Wāṣif, p. 273, and in the *Dīwān Abī Nuwās*. If these two lines are interpolations, they are excellent ones for the structure of the poem. I am using the text in Wāṣif, with the exception of line four, where I read *fa-buḥ bi-smi man tahwā* (instead of *ahwā*) with Ahlwardt and *Dīwān Abī Nuwās*. Line two in Wāṣif is more fluent than in *Dīwān Abī Nuwās*, where there is a forced effort at symmetry, and in line six Wāṣif's *bi-ḳulli aḳhī qaṣfin* seems better than *bi-ḳullī aḳhī fatḳin* in *Dīwān Abī Nuwās*, where *fatḳin* is repeated from the previous line.

or against secrecy:

(4) fa-buḥ bi-smi man tahwā wa-da'nī mina l-kunā
fa-lā khayra fī l-ladhdhāti min dūnihā sitru

Reveal the name of the one you love, and let me be done with allusions, because there is no good in veiled pleasures.

Line five continues this type of syntax (no *A* unless *B*), but while the syntax makes for continuity, the words broaden the stage and begin a transition:

(5) wa-lā khayra fī fatkin bi-dūni majānatin
wa-lā fī mujūnin laysa yatba'uhū kufru
(6) bi-kulli akhī qaṣfin ka-anna jabīnahū
hilālun wa-qad ḥaffat bihi l-anjumu z-zuhru
(7) wa-khammāratin nabbahtuhā ba'da haj'atin
wa-qad ghābati l-jawzā'u wa-nḥadara n-nasru

And there is no good in temerity without licentiousness, nor in licentiousness without impiety to top it off, / with companions, each a reveler whose brow is like a crescent moon, having been encircled by bright stars. / And the wineseller(s) I roused after their first slumber, when Orion was gone and Aquila had set! ...

The rest of the poem, appropriately enough, is an idyll of licentiousness. The composition is of a type favored by Abū Nuwās and imitated in the wine poems of his followers, in which a direct statement by the poet—on anything from spring lightheadedness to drink as a panacea for gloom—is balanced and followed by a wine-drinking scene with its standard topoi. The transition between the two parts is most frequently hinged upon the *waw rubba*.

In our poem the passage from the first part to the second is fluent and subtle. Each of the first four lines is an independent syntactic unit: lop off the connectives and each will make a sentence by itself. The fifth line still retains the syntactic pattern that characterizes the opening, but it flows on into line six with the *bi-* (with companions, etc.). This leisurely double-length proposition is a syntactic flirtation: its length, set in relief, delays coming to the idyll; its content promises to do so. In this way, the recognition of the cliché "winesellers I roused," which introduces the tavern scene, becomes a moment of pleasure, and it is followed by a second pleasure when we notice how smooth and elegant the transition is rendered by the *wa-qad* clauses immediately before and after the break: the stellar metaphor and the stellar description of the actual time of night.

The poem *li-ḍaw'i barqin* illustrates in an intriguing fashion the role that *waw rubba* plays in abrupt transitions. For our purposes, the most striking thing about the poem is that it would fly apart if it were not full of a variety of echoes and symmetries. It is composed in such a way that sections without introductory markers alternate three times with sections that open with *waw rubba* followed by an asyndetic relative clause (*ṣifa*). Each time, the *waw rubba* brings a change of scene. The new scene may serve as an example or an explanation, but the precise nature of the connection is left to the reader's imagination. The following, in which the first word of each section is in italics, will sketch the progression of the poem:

(1) *li-ḍaw'i* barqin ẓaliltu mukta'ibā
shaqqa sanāhū fī l-jawwi wa-ltahabā
(2) yūmiḍu fī ḍāḥiki n-nawājidhi . . .

I passed the day in grief at the gleam of lightning whose brilliance made a rent in the air as it shot straight down and burst into flame, / flashing in the form of teeth in laughter . . .

(4) *wa-nāʾiḥin* habba fī l-ghuṣūni ḍuḥan
li-muntashin mawhinan idhā nqalabā
(5) yadʿū bi-dhikrin ʿalā smihī li-hawan
yudhkiruhū fī zamānihi r-ruṭubā

And the moaning dove that started among the branches, in the morning, because someone drunk since midnight turned over on to his other side, / and blessed a beloved person, invoking God for his sake, a beloved who reminds him of spring plants.

(6) *fa-bittu* mithla l-muqīmi mughtariban
yadʿū bi-wāwaylatā wa-wāḥarabā

So I remained all night like one stopping on his way to a strange land, crying out "alas!" and "woe!"

(10) *wa-fityatin* lā l-mirāʾu yashmuluhum . . .

And good fellows, never engaged in strife. . . . [*The next six lines, which are in the middle of the poem, form a miniature wine-song, complete with the stock motifs of the saki and the mixing of wine and water.*]

(16) qālū wa-qad ankarū murāwaghatī l-
kaʾsa wa-qatlī bi-baththiya ṭ-ṭarabā
(17) *mā laka* am mā dahāka waylaka mā
ghālaka ḥattā nfaradta muktaʾibā

They said, having disapproved of me for fighting off the cup and for killing pleasure with my grief: / "What is the matter with you? Or has something just come upon you? Woe to you, whatever can it be that has seized you so you keep to yourself, moping?..."

(22) *wa-ānisin* lā amallu majlisahū
qāma li-waqtin danā li-yanqalibā
(23) āthartu an lā yulāma ḥilmī ʻalā
ladhdhati qalbī fa-stashʻara l-waṣabā
(24) fa-rāḥa lā ʻuṭṭilathu ʻāfiyatun
wa-bāta ṭarfī min ṭarfihī junubā

And some courteous person whose company would never bore me, who arose as the time approached for him to return . . . / I preferred keeping my self-control [ḥilm] *blameless to the pleasure of my heart, and my heart became filled with agony. / So he went—may no manner of wellbeing be denied him—and my glances remained far from his all night.*[10] [*end*]

The rhyming supports this arrangement in six sections. Of the lines that begin new sections but do not start with *waw rubba,* line six has internal rhyme before the caesura (the only such rhyme after the customary one in the first line), and line seventeen repeats the internal rhyme-word of line one, *mukta'ibā.* Of the lines that do begin with *waw rubba,* the first and third (vss. 4 and 22) use different forms of the same verb as rhyme-words: *inqalabā* and *yanqalibā.* It is part of the arrangement that in the last line "my glances remained far from his all night" returns us to the first line, "I passed the day in grief at the gleam of lightning." The emphasis on see-

[10] *Dīwān Abī Nuwās,* 38-39; Ahlwardt, *Diwan,* no. 9. In line 22, *yanqalibā* may be a double-entendre. In line 24, both Ahlwardt and *Dīwān Abī Nuwās* read *'aṭṭalathu.* The passive seems more likely to me; cf. Reckendorf, *Arabische Syntax* (Heidelberg, 1921), 90.

ing, and the complementary contrast between *ẓaliltu*, "I passed the day," and *bāta*, "passed the night," close the circle.

The various types of formal arrangement order ostensibly discrete parts. The basic effect of the poem is achieved by sudden jumps, by the abrupt changes of scene in the lines with *waw rubba*. In practical terms De Goeje was certainly right in suggesting such phrases of linkage as "I remember," etc., for translating this *wa-*, but one must keep in mind the essential syntactic property of the construction: the particle *wa-* introduces a phrase without a predicate. It stands before a noun that is followed by a descriptive relative clause, but there is no predication:

wa-nā'iḥin habba fī l-ghuṣūni ḍuḥan . . .

And the moaning dove that started in the branches in the morning . . .

In the Arabic there is no "I remember a dove," or "Then there was a dove." The *waw rubba* is deictic, but it does no more than point; it is as if it pushed a fresh slide into the projector. The gesture of pointing then takes the place of intellectual mediation, which is left to the reader. The last three lines of our poem show that even the exact position of a scene can be ambiguous: the final episode may be the end of the party described, or else the person mentioned in line 22 may be the cause of the poet's original melancholy. The general sequence would support the first interpretation, and the blessing in the last line the latter. The gaps in continuity suppress the perspective of the author's mind, and we seem to get random associations, the jumble of memory. It is one of the characteristics of the type of poetry we are dealing with that most of the lyrics are hung on the poet's "I," but the "I" often does not order the phenomena. The hoops of poetic form—internal references that cut across the linear sequence, or distinct compositional patterns—keep the superficially disparate parts together, and create a self. Under their pressure the gaps between parts become a source of echoes. The paradoxical relation between this formal self and the discontinuity among the things that the self remembers endows the poetry with the poignancy of the instant, with the fascination of the dancer under stroboscopic lights.

Because of their importance for Abū Nuwās's compositional technique, I will discuss some further examples of the use of internal cross references. Let us first look at the wine poem that begins with the line

a-mā yasurruka anna l-arḍa zahrā'u
wal-khamru mumkinatun shamṭā'u 'adhrā'u[11]

Does it not cheer you that the earth is in bloom, while the wine is there for the taking, old and virginal?

This piece happens to be of the same two-part pattern as *a-lā fa-sqinī khamran*, although the second section begins with *yā rubba* rather than the more usual *wa-*. The first part of the poem celebrates spring in the gardens of Karkh. Birds sing on the trees:

(5) idhā taghannayna lā yubqīna jāniḥatan
illā bihā ṭarabun yushfā bihi d-dā'u

When they sing they leave no heart without the delight that cures sickness.

The cure-all motif, which also belongs to wine poetry, serves as a hint of transition to the wine-house idyll that begins here:

[11] *Dīwān Abī Nuwās*, 14; translation (sporadically different from mine) in Wagner, *Abū Nuwās*, 293.

(6) yā rubba manzili khammārin aṭaftu bihī
wal-laylu ḥullatuhū kal-qāri sawdā'u

O the many houses of wine merchants I have circumambulated, while the garments of the night were pitch black!

The second part contains a dialogue. The poem ends by mentioning a singing girl and her song:

kam qad taghannat wa-lā lawmun yulimmu binā
da' 'anka lawmī fa-inna l-lawma ighrā'u

How often she sang, while no word of blame could get at us: "Leave off blaming me, for blame only urges one on!"

As it happens, the quoted snippet of song also comes from Abū Nuwās. The remarkable thing is the repetition of the verb *taghannā,* "to sing." As the recurrent words did in the last poem, here the phrases "they sing" and "they sang" coordinate otherwise separate scenes. The contents become delinearized; the spring scene and the drinking scene are suddenly superimposed in a way that enriches both.

De-linearization of this kind is the basic technique in one of the finest pieces in Abū Nuwās's *dīwān*. The poem opens with a variation on the deserted-dwelling motif:[12]

(1) 'afā l-muṣallā wa-aqwati l-kuthubu
minniya fal-mirbadāni fal-lababu
(2) fal-masjidu l-jāmi'u l-murū'ati wad-
dīni 'afā faṣ-ṣiḥānu far-raḥabu

[12] *Dīwān Abī Nuwās*, 32; Ahlwardt, *Diwan*, no. 6; translations in Wagner, *Abū Nuwās*, 297 and R. A. Nicholson, *Translations of Eastern Poetry and Prose* (Cambridge, 1922), 31-32.

Effaced is Muṣallā, the dunes have been deserted by me, and also Mirbad and Labab; / and the mosque that brought together manliness and piety is effaced, and the courtyards and the public squares . . .

These two lines work as well as they do through several echo effects punctuating the quick, harsh succession of "and" clauses. The second "effaced" comes unexpectedly, at a point of minimal stress, where it manages to be purely emotive because it is not needed for information. The quasi-merism that follows it is both an afterthought and a reverberation that completes the deepening impression of desolation. In line four, attention shifts to the poet's old companions:

(3) manāzilun qad ʿamartuhā yafaʿan
ḥattā badā fī ʿidhāriya sh-shahabu
(4) fī fityatin kas-suyūfi hazzahumū
sharkhu shabābin wa-zānahum adabu

Places I inhabited as a young man, until gray showed in the beard on my cheeks, / among fine fellows like swords brandished by the vigor of youth, adorned by polite culture.

The phrase *fī fityatin kas-suyūfi* is a cliché, and in the reader acquainted with the tradition it activates a mental set so that he now expects a new scene of wine or love poetry involving the companions. The shock is all the greater when these expectations are cut off in the very next line:

(5) thumma arāba z-zamānu fa-qtasamū
aydī sabā fī l-bilādi fa-nshaʿabū

Then Time brought its vicissitudes, and they dispersed like the people of Saba in the lands, and went their various ways.

The old days are gone for good:

(7) lammā tayaqqantu anna rawḥatahum
laysa lahā mā ḥayītu munqalabu
(8) ablaytu ṣabran lam yublihī aḥadun
wa-qtasamatnī ma'āribun shu'abu

When I realized with certainty that their departure was irreversible no matter how long I lived, / I tested patience as no one has, and various desires divided me among themselves.

This is a transition to the wine poem proper that takes up the rest of the piece, but while the transition pulls one way, the words *wa-qtasamatnī,* "divided me," and *shu'abu,* "various," recall line five, the original state of mind that will not let go. One even wonders whether there is a hidden pun here on *ma'ārib,* "desires," and *Ma'rib,* the place of the catastrophe remembered in the proverb "They dispersed like the people of Saba." A long conceit follows, elaborating the notion that the poet becomes a child to the vine since no permanent relationships are possible among people. The movement towards a conclusion begins with the description of drinking cups. There is a chain of motifs: golden wine and gold cups—the cups are engraved with figures above whom the wine is like a sky—the bubbles in the wine are the stars—and then the last line follows:

(25) ka-annahā lu'lu'un tubaddiduhū
aydī 'adhārā afḍā bihā l-la'ibu

As though they were pearls that the hands of virgins, who have grown exuberant at play, scatter.

Our poem ends with a stock simile; it is resolved by the convention "bubbles" = "pearls." But far more happens than just that: with the exultant final image we are suddenly back at *fa-qtasamū aydī sabā* (line five) and the desolation of the opening. The two verbs meaning "scatter" (*iqtasamū* vs. *tubaddidu*) are of different roots, but their position in the line is the same, and they are of course semantically linked. In both lines, the second half begins with *aydī*. The girls scatter pearls; men scatter. The difference of voice between *iqtasamū* (middle) and *tubaddidu* (active) sets the tone: man is reduced to a plaything purely acted upon. It is important that the sentences that effect this montage are both conventional: the first a proverb, the second (bubbles = pearls) a stock simile. The conventions, weighted with their permanence, echo the laws of experience in the poem. They act out the unchanging on the stage of language.

To conclude, here is an example in which the reticulation of invention and convention gives the poem its coherence and characteristic tone:[13]

wajhu ḥamdāna fa-ḥdharū -
hū kitābu z-zanādiqah
fīhi ashyā'u yaz'umu n -
nāsu bil-qalbi 'āliqah
man ra'āhū fa-nafsuhū
naḥwahu d-dahra tā'iqah
kullamā ftarra ḍāḥikan
qultu īmāḍu bāriqah

Watch out! Ḥamdān's face is the Manicheans' book. / People claim that there are things in it that cling to the heart. / Whoever sees him, his soul will forever crave after him. / Each time he parts his lips in laughter, I say: "Flash of lightning from a storm cloud."

[13] *Dīwān Abī Nuwās,* 448.

This is a fairly unambitious poem, but it illustrates how a conventional phrase works as resolution and at the same time has a life of its own. The charged line in the quatrain is the first. It contains a striking proposition that is expanded and elaborated upon in the next two lines. The fourth line, on the other hand, is pure formula. The word *iftarra* alone conjures up the traditional comparison between the flash of lightning and the gleam of the laughing beauty's teeth. The cliché anchors the passage around it in the poetic tradition. We see time and time again that this kind of anchoring, far from being simple stuffing, must have been felt a necessary follow-up of invention by the contemporary sensibility, somewhat as a series of variations in music may end with the original theme.

At the same time, the last line picks up some of the major strands in the quatrain. The overtones of *bāriqa*, "lightning cloud," which lead to its technical use for the beginning of revelation or mystical inspiration, link up with *Manicheans' book* (*zanādiqa* definitely meaning "Manicheans" in this passage) and with the seduced soul. There is another overtone that works at a more concrete level since one of the connotations of *bāriqa* is "beautiful person."[14] The association of physical beauty too connects with the Manicheans' book, since their books were famous for their handsome appearance.[15] Thus the last line participates in the fusion of the soul's and the heart's seduction, besides bringing the poem to a rest.

[14] Cf. Tha'ālibī, *Kitāb an-nihāya fī t-ta'rīḍ wal-kināya* (Mecca, 1884), 17.

[15] See for example al-Jāḥiẓ, *Ḥayawān*, I, 55-56.

five
Ambiguities

In the poems I will now consider, various forms of sustained ambiguity provide complexity as well as coherence. The three pieces—a short poem by Abū Nuwās, Abū Tammām's celebrated ode upon the conquest of Amorium,[1] and an elegy by al-Mutanabbī—reveal subtleties, the recognition of which may improve our habits in reading Arabic verse. The first and third exhibit neat formal organizations. The first poem is characterized by puns that link two sets of ideas; the second poem depends on logical and emotional ambiguities that arise from the use of paronomasia; the third works its way towards strange and disturbing alliances of connotation.

When I speak of formal organization, I do not mean that the poet was necessarily conscious of a grid that could be abstracted from the poem, but I do suggest that a poetry that does not use the guideline of a plot will tend to create formal arrangements of its matter and that such arrangements can frequently be observed in Arabic verse.

1

The first example is short enough to quote in full:[2]

1 al-jismu minnī saqīmun shaffahu n-naṣabu
wal-qalbu dhū lawʿatin kan-nāri taltahibu

[1] My opinions about the workings of paronomasia in this poem have changed considerably since my somewhat inadequate essay on the subject in *JSS*, XII (1967), 83-90.

[2] *Dīwān Abī Nuwās*, 64.

2 innī hawītu ḥabīban lastu adhkuruhū
illā tabādara mā'u l-'ayni yansakibu
3 al-badru ṣūratuhū wash-shamsu jabhatuhū
wa-lil-ghazālati minhu l-'aynu wal-lababu
4 muzannarun yatamashshā naḥwa bī'atihī
ilāhuhu l-ibnu fīmā qāla waṣ-ṣulubu
5 yā laytanī l-qassu aw muṭrānu bī'atihī
aw laytanī 'indahu l-injīlu wal-kutubu
6 aw laytanī kuntu qurbānan yuqarribuhū
aw ka'sa khamratihī aw laytanī l-ḥababu
7 kaymā afūza bi-qurbin minhu yanfa'unī
wa-yanjalī saqamī wal-baththu wal-kurabu

1 *My body is diseased, gaunt with grief, while my heart flutters, blazing like fire.*
2 *I love a beloved whom I never think of without tears hastening to flow.*
3 *His face is the full moon; his forehead is the sun; his eyes and neck are a gazelle's.*
4 *Wearing the girdle of the Christians, he walks towards his church. The Son—as he claimed—is his God, and* [*he also prays to*] *the crucifixes.*
5 *If only I were the priest, or the metropolitan of his church, or else his* [*the celebrant's*] *Gospel and Bible;*
6 *Or if only I were the sacrifice he offers* [*i.e., communion*] *or his cup of wine, or a bubble in the wine;*
7 *So that I might get to be near him* [*the communicant*], *which would do me good, and so that my disease, grief, and anxiety might clear away.*

The poem is quite conventional. The first two lines set up the common enough antithesis that clamps together a burning heart and a watering eye; the third is purely descriptive and almost wholly formulaic. The next verse tells us that the poet is languishing on account of a Christian boy. This is essential for what is to follow, but, still, it only helps fill in the backdrop. The next three lines bear the matter of the poem. The coda arches back to the beginning: *yanjalī saqamī*, "so that my disease might clear away," echoes *saqīm*, "diseased." As is often the case, both beginning and end are made fast to tradition by conventional phrasing. Compare the similar verse by Dhū r-Rumma:[3]

innī akhū l-jismi fīhi s-suqmu wal-kurabu . . .

I have the kind of body in which there are disease and anxieties . . .

A formal contrast divides Abū Nuwās's poem into three parts: verses 1-4; the central block comprising verses 5-7a; and the coda, 7b. The contrast is brought about by the alternation of catalogue types. The enumerations in verses three and four are, so to speak, lateral: the various descriptions may simultaneously apply to a single object—"His forehead is the sun; his eyes and neck a gazelle's," etc. In turn, the optatives in the middle section form a replacive series, since no one can be metropolitan and bubble at the same time. The concluding half-line is again lateral: disease, grief, and anxiety would all vanish together.

The formal buttressing of the poem is not without bearing upon the contents. The arch that links the opening statement to the coda also directs our attention to the rest of the vocabulary in the first and last lines. As *saqīm* is opposed to *yanjalī saqamī*, so *wal-qalbu dhū law'atin kan-nāri taltahibu*, "my heart flutters, blazing like fire," contrasts with *kaymā afūza bi-qurbin minhu*, "that I might obtain his nearness." The for-

[3] *The Dīwān of Ghailān ibn 'Uqbah known as Dhū 'r-Rummah*, ed. C. H. H. Macartney (Cambridge, 1919), 7.

mal relation between the two phrases brings to prominence a feature common to both: the possession of religious overtones. These overtones might be judged indistinct if the weighted words occurred in isolation, but their conjunction makes the echoes ring clear. "The fire" often means hellfire in Arabic. *Fāza* is frequently used in the Koran in the sense of obtaining a place in Paradise, and the people who are lucky enough to get in tend to be contrasted with those who end up in the flames.[4] This sense of *fāza* is sufficiently strong for the verb to be understood, in religious contexts, without the help of a grammatical object or other complement. For the kind of nearness in which anxiety and grief pass away, compare the *ḥadīth* (saying ascribed to Mohammed): "God, who is great and glorious, has worshipers who are neither prophets nor martyrs, but whom the prophets and martyrs consider happy on account of their places [*majālisihim*] and their nearness to God [*qurbihim mina l-lāh*]. . . . People will be in terror on the day of resurrection, but they will feel no terror; for they are God's friends, for whom there is no fear and no anxiety to suffer."[5]

In the kind of nearness that our lover craves, it is not only the hellfire in the heart that is extinguished; the suppliant's whole being is put out. The poet, while poaching upon reli-

[4] The contrast is all the more natural, since one of the meanings of *fāza* is to find safety from danger. This sense is often brought out in sermons, cf. Ibn 'Abdrabbihi, *Kitāb al-'iqd al-farīd*, ed. Aḥ. Amīn, Aḥ. az-Zayn, and Ibr. al-Abyārī (Cairo, 1949-1965), IV, 106: *man najā yawma'idhin fa-qad fāza*; Ibn Nubāta, *Dīwān ḳhuṭab b. Nubāta*, ed. Ṭ. al-Jazā'irī (Beirut, 1894), 21: *al-fawza bi-jiwāri r-raḥmān*.

[5] Aḥmad ibn Ḥanbal, *Musnad* (Cairo, 1895), V, 343. The word for anxiety is *hamm*, which, like *ḳurba*, can refer to day-to-day worries as well as to the anxiety at the last judgment. For *ḳurba* in both senses, cf. Bukhārī, *Ṣaḥīḥ*, *maẓālim*, 3: *man farraja 'an muslimin ḳurbatan farraja l-lāhu 'anhu ḳurbatan min ḳurabāti yawmi l-qiyāma.*

gious experience, anticipates a later form of his game. Thus, for example, as-Sarrāj explains an obscure saying of Shiblī's by pointing out that the mystic feels himself blotted out while he contemplates the nearness of his Master.[6] In turn, the poet's play with metaphor is taken up by the mystic, who must give words new meanings because he has a fixed sacred text to which he must relate his experience. Compare Shiblī, who thought hell was separation from God: "What shall I make of 'blazing and scorching'? To my mind, the phrase 'blazing and scorching; you will dwell in it' means 'in a state of being cut off and shunned.'"[7] Ascetics among Abū Nuwās's contemporaries perhaps held no mystical notions, but they would at any rate have agreed with the poem's principle that weeping and terror end only with death.

The poet succeeds in his mimicry of a religious progression chiefly through the increasing humility in the central sequence of optatives. The successive incarnations go from the authoritarian to the powerless but intimate. There is a piquancy, of course, in the yoking together of Christian things and Islamic echoes, but it is not all. There is also a second surface to the poem, and it is a crooked mirror to the first surface of tender devotion. It depends on the presence of punning words in the middle section.

First, *yā laytanī l-qassu aw muṭrānu bī'atihī*, "if only I were the priest, or the metropolitan of his church." The evidence for taking this phrase as a double-entendre is very strong. According to a medieval dictionary of allusions, *qass* and *bī'a* (or *dayr*) go together in a slang phrase for sexual intercourse.[8] Badī' az-Zamān al-Hamadhāni quotes a poem by Abū

[6] Abū Naṣr as-Sarrāj, *Kitāb al-luma' fī t-taṣawwuf*, ed. R. A. Nicholson (London, 1914), 396.

[7] *Luma'*, 406.

[8] Aḥ. ibn Muḥ. al-Jurjānī th-Thaqafī, *al-Muntakhab min kināyāt al-udabā' wa-ishārāt al-bulaghā'* (Cairo, 1908), 19.

Nuwās, which he considers worthy of having been inspired by the devil himself, and which includes the verses:

wa-zurtu maḍja'ahū qabla ṣ-ṣabāḥi wa-qad
dallat 'alā ṣ-ṣubḥi aṣwātu n-nawāqīsi
fa-qāla man dhā fa-qultu l-qassu zāra wa-lā
buddun li-dayrika min tashmīsi qissīsi[9]

I visited his bed just before morning, when dawn had been announced by the sound of gongs. / He said: "Who is it?" I said: "The priest has come to visit; your monastery must have the ministrations of priests."

In the next line, "if only I were the sacrifice he offers" is built on a pun. Once again, internal evidence is available; for Abū Nuwās himself uses the word *qurbān* in an obviously sensual context:

bi-fityānin yarawna l-qat- la fil-ladhdhāti qurbānā[10]

With young men who consider it a sacrifice to be killed with pleasure ...

Side by side with the quasi-ascetic tone, there is an unabashed sexual innuendo in the poem. We need not jump over the fence and hold that the presence of such an innuendo turns the primary surface of the poem into a joke. Rather, the possessor of the slangy goatish voice manages to tenant one body together with the charming and tender speaker proper to the 'Udhrī *ghazal*, and with the advocate of quasi-religious self-effacement.

Such are the contradictions on which Abū Nuwās's poetry thrives.

[9] *Maqāmāt*, 270. The attribution may be erroneous.
[10] *Dīwān Abī Nuwās*, 613.

2

The pun unfolded becomes paronomasia, *tajnīs*. As rhetorical figures go, paronomasia has had varied fortunes. Quintilian, for example, quotes several instances of it; he turns up his nose at most, but stoops to consider it reasonably elegant when used for the sake of contrast.[11] *Tajnīs* is among the standard devices in medieval Arabic rhetoric, but the critics advise poets to use it sparingly, and many find fault with Abū Tammām's excessive predilection for this kind of ornament.

Āmidī, in his essay of comparison between Abū Tammām and Buḥturī, has a separate section headed "Cases of displeasing paronomasia in the poetry of Abū Tammām."[12] He points out that *tajnīs* was a figure of rhetoric known to the old poets, who could be trusted not to go overboard with it, and that Abū Tammām misguidedly made it his chief poetic instrument. Bāqillānī chides Abū Tammām for artificiality, *takalluf*.[13] Jurjānī gives several examples of forced word play in Abū Tammām's work, although he does adduce passages in which *tajnīs* is applied to advantage.[14] Much of this criticism is just. We need only consider the verse quoted by both Āmidī and Jurjānī:

qarrat bi-*qurrāna* 'aynu d-dīni wa-*shtatarat*
bil-*ashtarayni* 'uyūnu sh-shirki fa-ṣtulimā[15]

At Qurrān, *the eye of the Faith was* soothed, *and at* Ashtarān *the eyes of polytheism became* diseased [*lit.*,

[11] *Institutio Oratoria*, IX.iii.70-71.

[12] *al-Muwāzana bayn shi'r Abī Tammām wal-Buḥturī*, ed. Aḥ. Ṣaqr (Cairo, 1961-1965), I, 265.

[13] Cf. G. E. von Grunebaum, *A Tenth Century Document of Arabic Literary Theory* (Chicago, 1950), 51-52.

[14] *Asrār al-balāgha*, ed. H. Ritter (Istanbul, 1954), 15.

[15] *Muwāzana*, I, 268; *Asrār*, 16.

afflicted with inversion of the margins of the eyelids] so that it was uprooted.

This is admittedly too clever by half. The metaphor is too shallow to sustain the cleverness, and the verse is crippled. But Abū Tammām could also be master of his rhetoric, as a look at one of his celebrated compositions will show.[16]

The poem was written in praise of al-Mu'taṣim's conquest of Amorium in 838. Its contents can be summarized as follows:

vss. 1-12: The Muslim swords have disproved the astrologers' predictions, who thought the time inauspicious for conquest.
vss. 13-22: The city, which had never before been taken, is compared to a woman.
vss. 23-35: Description of the devastation; the fire in the city.
vss. 36-49: Description and praise of the caliph.
vss. 50-61: Contrasting description of the Byzantine emperor Theophilus. His flight.
vss. 62-66: Further description of the siege, and of the women captured by the victors.
vss. 67-71: Praise of the caliph and of the victory.

Tajnīs is used throughout, but the reader cannot fail to be struck by the way it is clustered in two passages: verses 1-3 and 63-66. The first three lines are:

1 as-sayfu aṣdaqu inbā'an mina l-kutubi
fī *ḥaddihi* l-*ḥaddu* bayna l-jiddi wal-la'ibi
2 bīḍu ṣ-*ṣafā'iḥi* lā sūdu ṣ-*ṣaḥā'ifi* fī
mutūnihinna jalā'u sh-shakki war-riyabi

[16] See *Dīwān Abī Tammām*, ed., with Tibrīzī's comm., Muḥ. 'Abduh 'Azzām (Cairo, 1951-1957), 1, 45-79.

3 wal-ʿilmu fī *shuhubi* l-armāḥi lāmiʿatan
bayna l-khamīsayni lā fī s-sabʿati sh-*shuhubi*

1 The sword is more truthful in its information than writings are in theirs; the boundary *between seriousness and play is in the sword's* edge.
2 The clearing up of doubt and uncertainty lies in the faces of white broadswords, *not in the texts on black* pages.
3 And knowledge comes from the flaring *up of lances as they flash between two fivefold armies, not from the seven* heavenly bodies.

The contrast between knowledge, which is gained from the clear-cut results of battles, and the astrologers' writings is established by a series of plays on words. The most charged single word in the passage is *mutūnihinna*, which combines references to the swords (*matn*, "the broad side of a sword") and the writings (*matn*, "text"). Two objects of experience are brought together by means of a verbal coincidence, while their context puts them in contrast. A similar conflict of forces is at work in the juxtaposition of *ṣafāʾiḥ*, "broadswords," and *ṣaḥāʾif*, "pages." The subtle phonetic difference in these words is complemented by the fact that they have identical grammars (genitives following construct forms), but go with opposites: *bīḍ*, "white," and *sūd*, "black." The third line is not unlike in technique. *Shuhub*, "flare," and *shuhub*, "heavenly bodies," have the same acoustic form, but here there is a contrast in the arrangement of the qualifying words: *fī shuhubi l-armāḥi* in the first hemistich, *fī s-sabʿati sh-shuhubi* in the second. Introducing all of this, we find what may be called a conjunctive use of *tajnīs* in the first verse: *fī ḥaddihi l-ḥaddu*, "the boundary is in its edge," links together two objects both phonetically and logically.

It is clear why the opposition set up in verses 1-3 is important. Al-Muʿtaṣim, the hero, is represented historically as acting against dark predictions and religiously as acting with God against falsehood. The contrast between light and dark (verse two), day and night (verse three), is picked up in verse seven:

> wa-khawwafū n-nāsa min dahyā'a muẓlimatin . . .
>
> *And they [the astrologers] made people fear a dark catastrophe . . .*

The light-dark opposition is developed along with the idea of disclosing, or unveiling, which, in its variations and expansions, gives the poem its framework. The idea appears at the very beginning, with the word *jalā'*, "clearing up," in verse two. It returns in verse thirty, in the middle of Abū Tammām's description of the destruction of Amorium:

> taṣarraḥa d-dahru taṣrīḥa l-ghamāmi lahā . . .
>
> *Destiny became clear to her, as clouds clear from the sun . . . .*

This verse is preceded by a description of the confusion of light and darkness caused by the fires which shone by night and the smoke which then obscured the dawn. The *tajnīs al-ishtiqāq* (playing on different derivates of the same root) simply holds together the aspects of the ensuing disclosure: the physical dispersion of clouds, and the revelation of historical truth, the destined Muslim victory.

The next version of unveiling comes in the description of the caliph, al-Mu'taṣim, in verse thirty-eight:

> wa-muṭ'ami n-naṣri lam takham asinnatuhū
> yawman wa-lā ḥujibat 'an rūḥi muḥtajibi . . .

> *One used to feeding on victory, whose spearpoint has never been dulled, nor hindered from access to the soul of any protected* [*enemy*] . . .

The passive verb *ḥujibat* simply means "hindered," and the participle *muḥtajib*, in the context, "one protected" or "seeking concealment," but the paronomasia conjures up associations of the other and basic meaning of the root, namely "veiling." Thus the verse links up with the general theme of disclosing, and, more specifically, it recalls the metaphor of the city as a woman from verses 15-22. The end of the poem picks up these allusions and metaphors. As at the beginning, the clustering of *tajnīs* goes hand in hand with clustered images of light and unveiling.

Here, in lines 63-66, after having described the defeat of the Byzantines, Abū Tammām gathers up the images of light and disclosure in a passage about the captured women:

63 kam nīla taḥta *sanāhā* min *sanā* qamarin
wa-taḥta *'āriḍihā* min *'āriḍin* sanibi
64 kam kāna fī qaṭ'i *asbābi* r-riqābi bihā
ilā l-mukhaddarati l-'adhrā'i min *sababi*
65 kam aḥrazat *quḍubu* l-hindīyi muṣlatatan
tahtazzu min *quḍubin tahtazzu* fī kuthubi
66 *bīḍun* idhā ntuḍiyat min *ḥujbihā* raja'at
aḥaqqa bil-*bīḍi* atrāban mina l-*ḥujubi*

63 *Many a moon's* resplendence *was gained under its* [*the war's*] glare, *and many a white* tooth *under its* cloud.
64 *Many were the* ways *to sequestered virgins through cutting necks like so many* strings.
65 *The Indian* swords *that* quivered *unsheathed won many a* branch quivering *on a sandhill* [*a woman with a narrow waist and substantial foundations to it*].

66 *When the* white *swords that have been drawn from their* sheaths *return, they have a better claim to the women with* white-*bodied playmates than* veils *have.*

I will return to this cluster after a look at the conclusion of the ode, verse seventy-one:

abqat banī l-*aṣfari* l-mimrāḍi ka-smihimū
ṣufra l-wujūhi wa-jallat awjuha l-'arabi

They [*these battle-days*] *have left the sons of sickly* al-Aṣfar [*the Byzantines*] pale-faced, *befitting their name, but they have brightened the faces of the Arabs.*

The *tajnīs* proper here is a piece of mockery made from the position of superiority built up over seventy lines. That the verb used to describe the Arabs is *jallat*, "brightened," derived from the same root as *jalā'*, "clearing up," "disclosing," used in the second verse, is on the other hand a kind of hidden pun that comments on the structure of the poem.

Let us take a sentence of Jurjānī's as our next stepping stone: *fa-innaka lā tajidu tajnīsan maqbūlan . . . ḥattā yakūna l-ma'nā huwa l-ladhī ṭalabahu wa-stad'āhu wa-sāqa naḥwahu*, "you will find only such instances of *tajnīs* satisfactory as are required, called for, and led up to by the idea of the passage."[17] If we can manage to put aside suspicions of barbarous pomp or jejune verbal juggling, and feel pleased by the opening cluster of paronomasias as well as by verses 63-66, can we also establish some kind of direct relation between idea and rhetorical figure? The undertaking is hazardous, because nowadays we tend to think of rhetorical devices as flourishes and alarums with no content of their own and therefore as incapable of being more suited to one idea than

[17] *Asrār*, 10.

to another. But this is thinking with our taste. To take an obvious example, the symmetry of a chiasmus is its content, and the literary phenomenologist can work on the applications of this content in various texts.

Like all rhetorical figures, paronomasia is a linguistic anomaly. After all, good fences make good neighbors, and good phonetic distinctions among words promote comprehension of a sentence. At the same time, there is in language a tendency for semantic bonds to occasion some degree of analogous phonetic patterning; compare English *female* [fi:meyl], which replaces the expected [fem^{e}l] (cf. French *femelle*) due to analogy with [meyl]; or Arabic semantic-class patterns like *uḥdūtha*, "story," *uqṣūṣa*, "story," etc. This tendency, which is part of each speaker's linguistic equipment, underlies the psychological effect of paronomasia.

The pressure of semantic bonds on acoustic form translates into a myth: the myth of the rightness of naming, which E. R. Curtius called etymology as a catergory of thought.[18] The etymological myth was present in the Middle Ages not only in works of the learned—from Isidore's *Origines* to Midrashic hermeneutics—but also in spontaneous speech and poetry. Its simplest manifestation is in stories of the *nomen est omen* sort. Ibn Qutayba tells us, for instance, about a man who was declared an untrustworthy witness because he bore the peculiar name Abū Kuwayfir, understood as "Father of Little Infidel," and about 'Umar ibn 'Abdal'azīz's displeasure at a man unlucky enough to be called Ẓālim ibn Sarrāq, "Unjust, son of Thief."[19] A playful case of prognostication by (false) etymology is recorded in a passage of Ibn 'Abdrabbihi's, where al-Ash'ab requests a singing girl's ring for a keepsake. She puts him off with a quick reply: *Innahu* dhahabun *wa-*

[18] E. R. Curtius, *European Literature and the Latin Middle Ages*, transl. W. Trask (Princeton, 1953), 495-500.

[19] *Shi'r*, 17.

akhāfu an tadhhaba *wa-lākin khudh hādhā l-*ʿūda *fa-laʿallaka* taʿūd, "It is made of *gold* and I fear that you will *go away* from me. But take this *lute*—perhaps you will *come back* then."[20]

Abū Tammām's poem starts off with a *tajnīs* that does not impugn the myth: *fī ḥaddihi l-ḥaddu*, "in the sword's edge is the boundary." But this conjunction, expressed by *tajnīs,* is followed by disjunctions (the broadswords/not the pages, etc.) which are also expressed by *tajnīs.* Coming after *fī ḥaddihi l-ḥaddu,* the disjunctive use of paronomasia—that is to say: the affirmation that there are pairs of words *A* and *B* that sound alike but are such that *if A then not B*—amounts to an ambiguous view of the myth of naming. A muddle in our feelings towards language sets the stage here for the muddle that the swords' logic must clear up.

Now, in verses 63-66, all paronomasia is conjunctive: the structure of the paired words is *if A then B.* This is presented as historically true: the cloud of battle leads directly to the ladies' brilliant teeth; the éclat of spears is a means to the éclat of the women, and so on. The entire passage deals with just claims, proper acquisitions, and the like. Thus, we may say that the etymological myth is used faithfully and strictly. On the other hand, the objects that are joined—the violent and the voluptuous—form uneasy couples. More precisely, the conjunction has psychological validity, but we are not quite comfortable with it. In this section of the poem, then, there is an emotional ambivalence (for us as well as for Abū Tammām's courtly audience), although historically the conjunction is correct: by winning the battle, the Arabs did in fact capture the women.

To sum up, we can say that: in verses 1-3, the myth (that conjunction of sounds entails conjunction of referents) is am-

[20] *ʿIqd,* VI, 63.

biguous in view of the historical facts, since blades proved true and astrologers' books false, etc., while in verses 63-66, where the myth of conjunction is unambiguous in view of the facts, the specific conjunctions are emotionally ambiguous.

In these crucial clusters, therefore, we find something either logically or emotionally odd about the use of paronomasia. It is this very oddity that makes the passages work, because in it the basic linguistic character of paronomasia—oddity and subversion—comes into play.

We must also note that in the poem bundles of *tajnīs* occur together with bundles of "light/dark" and "veiled/unveiled" imagery, so that the antithetical imagery and the ambiguous character of *tajnīs* support and complement one another.

I would like to add, in passing, an example of the kind of gain that well-applied paronomasia can bring to the poet. Let us consider two lines again:

3 wal-'ilmu fī *shuhubi* l-armāḥi lāmi'atan
bayna l-khamīsayni lā fī s-sab'ati sh-*shuhubi*

And knowledge comes from the flaring up of lances as they flash between two fivefold armies, not from the seven heavenly bodies.

65 kam aḥrazat *quḍubu* l-hindīyi muṣlatatan
tahtazzu min *quḍubin* tahtazzu fī kuthubi

The Indian swords that quivered unsheathed won many a branch quivering on a sandhill.

The blazing light of spearpoints is a stock metaphor in Arabic poetry. So is the equation of women's hips and sandhills. In each of these verses, however, the cliché is paronomastically linked to another word that happens to be concrete: the stars (*shuhub*) and the swords (*quḍub*). These ties to the primary world invigorate the old conventions, by giving us a nudge and opening our eyes again to the worn metaphors' combinatory possibilities.

3

In my third example, a principle of composition is derived from ambiguities of connotation. The poem is an elegy commemorating the mother of al-Mutanabbī's patron, Sayfaddawla, ruler of Aleppo.[21] A great part of the imagery is supplied by series of variations on one focal ambivalence: the death-in-life theme: *wenn wir uns mitten im Leben meinen.* This is an ambiguity that is much used by gnostic and mystical literature in Islam;[22] in al-Mutanabbī's poem it is all the grimmer for not having a homiletic side. The elegy is much too long to quote in full. Its contents can be summarized as follows:

A (vss. 1-4) Gnomic introduction about the instability of all worldly things;
B (vss. 5-9) The poet is inured to misfortune, but this lady's death is a catastrophe of unprecedented magnitude;
C (vss. 10-21) The lady in the grave; her glorious position while alive; her boundless generosity;
D (vss. 22-27) The lady in the grave; her glorious son Sayfaddawla;
E (vss. 28-35) The lady in the grave; splendor of her funeral and the participants' grief;

[21] See Nāṣīf al-Yāzijī, *al-'Arf aṭ-ṭayyib fī sharḥ dīwān Abī ṭ-Ṭayyib* (Beirut, 1964), II, 19-25; *Dīwān Abī ṭ-Ṭayyib al-Mutanabbī*, ed., with comm. by Wāḥidī, Fr. Dieterici (Berlin, 1861), 388-95.

[22] For references, see Chapter VI, note 22.

F (vss. 36-38) Second gnomic passage (yudaffinu baʿḍunā baʾḍan, *"We go on burying each other," etc.*);

G (vss. 39-44) Encomium of Sayfaddawla in terms of his endurance in the face of misfortune.

Sections *A* and *B* are reflected in the concluding sections *F* and *G*. The middle passages *C*, *D* and *E* appear to be a set of variations. Each of the three consists of some version of the lady-in-the-grave image followed by a subsection representing some aspect of the nobility and magnificence surrounding her. What these panegyric subsections do is *reculer pour mieux sauter*. I quote the opening lines of sections *C*, *D* and *E*:

10 ṣalātu l-lāhi khāliqinā ḥanūṭun
ʿalā l-wajhi l-mukaffani bil-jamāli

The mercies of God, our Creator, are the balm upon the face that is shrouded in beauty.

22 nazalti ʿalā l-karāhati fī makānin
baʿudti ʿani n-nuʿāmā wash-shamāli

In spite of us you went down to a place where you are far from the south wind and the north.

28 wa-laysat kal-ināthi wa-lā l-lawātī
tuʿaddu lahā l-qubūru mina l-ḥijāli

She was not like other women; not like those for whom the grave is considered a curtained canopy.[23]

The grave is mentioned in the panegyric subsection of *C* a number of times (e.g., *yamurru bi-qabriki l-ʿāfī fa-yabkī*,

[23] Such as is set up for a bride.

"Seekers of beneficence pass by your grave and weep," etc.), but verse twenty-two is the first clear return to direct statement, just as verse ten is the first direct statement after the gnomic introduction. Verse twenty-eight is also a return to the affair immediately at hand after a short excursus on Sayfaddawla. The panegyric subsections of *C*, *D* and *E* deal respectively with the lady's own nobility, the glory of her surviving son, and the pomp of her funeral (*mashā l-umarā'u ḥawlayhā ḥufātan*, "Emirs walked barefoot around her bier," etc.). When only the burial is left to praise, the poem is near its goal.

In the gnomic introduction, the world is a loved but unattainable person (verses 3-4):

wa-man lam yaʿshaqi d-dunyā qadīman
wa-lākin lā sabīla ilā l-wiṣāli
naṣībuka fī ḥayātika min ḥabībin
naṣībuka fī manāmika min khayāli

Since the world began, has anyone been without passionate love for it? But there is no attaining a union of lovers. / Your share of the beloved, while you are alive, is just like your share of a phantom while you are asleep.

There is a poetic trick here. In pre-Islamic poetry, the elegy (*rithā'*) is distinguished from other types of *qaṣīda* by having no *nasīb*. The imagery of these two lines is, however, obviously taken from the *nasīb* and *ghazal* tradition. Such re-use of the vocabulary of love-poetry in a poem about death sets the theme that the poem will develop. The tone, to be sure, is also reminiscent of pious homilies. Man is foolishly infatuated with the world; earthly life is a space of sleep; the world is like a dream because all things lapse and none can be seized. But to warn is not the poet's purpose. He simply reaches into the prop-box of love poetry and invites shapes of death to put on the conventional lovers' masks.

Let us return to the first two lines of section *C*:

ṣalātu l-lāhi khāliqinā ḥanūṭun
'alā l-wajhi l-mukaffani bil-jamāli
'alā l-madfūni qabla t-turbi ṣawnan
wa-qabla l-laḥdi fī karami l-khilāli

The mercies of God, our Creator, are the balm upon the face that is shrouded in beauty, / upon one who had been buried in chastity before she descended into the dust, and in noble qualities before the tomb.

The words *ḥanūṭ*, "balm," and *mukaffan*, "shrouded," are made to do double duty. She is certainly wrapped in a shroud and embalmed with *ḥanūṭ*, but she is also embalmed with divine mercy and shrouded in beauty. There is a two-way pull here: mercy has to do with the world to come, but the beauty, presumably, is the beauty she possessed in this world. The first of these metaphors is all very well; the second is somewhat disturbing. If beauty can be a shroud in some cases —who knows? The *nasīb* to the world, which opened the elegy, is drawn closer to the mood of the story of the prince who makes love to a corpse, or to Rūmī's "How long will you love a dead beloved?"[24] The next line follows the same course. We are told that in some sense she was buried while alive, but it is a very pretty sense, being entombed in chastity and noble character traits. Only the similarity in phrasing to

[24] For the prince, see *Rasā'il Ikhwān aṣ-Ṣafā'* (Beirut, 1957), IV, 162-64. For "how long," see *Selected Poems from the Dīvāni Shamsi Tabrīz*, ed. and transl. R. A. Nicholson (Cambridge, 1898), 50-51: *tā kay kinār gīrī ma'shūq-i murde-rā.*

"shrouded in beauty" points in an uneasy direction; the metaphorical burial is now too near for comfort to the real thing: it is not only metaphor but also prefiguration.

The chill runs deeper in the first four lines of *D* (verses 22-25):

nazalti 'alā l-karāhati fī makānin
ba'udti 'ani n-nu'āmā wash-shamāli
tuḥajjabu 'anki rā'iḥatu l-khuzāmā
wa-tumna'u minki andā'u ṭ-ṭilāli
bi-dārin kullu sākinihā gharībun
ba'īdu d-dāri munbattu l-ḥibāli
ḥaṣānun mithlu mā'i l-muzni fīhī
katūmu s-sirri ṣādiqatu l-maqāli

In spite of us, you went down into a place where you are far from the south wind and the north. / The scent of lavender is veiled from you, and the soft rains cannot affect you, / in a house whose every tenant is a stranger, far away, his strings of affection snapped, / a house in which there is a person pure as rainwater, one who keeps secrets and speaks the truth.

The vocabulary of the traditional *ghazal* is prominent. The winds have a standard role in the supporting cast of the love poem: they carry messages to the beloved. The snapped strings of affection are stock-in-trade. Line twenty-five really stands things on their heads. One who keeps secrets is a standard expression of praise in the *ghazal*; its use to describe the dead is shockingly apposite. *Ṣādiqatu l-maqāli*, "one who speaks the truth," is again proper to the *ghazal*, but it also echoes the pious metaphor that the dead warn the living, as in Abū l-'Atāhiya's line:

wa-kānat fī ḥayātika lī ʿiẓātun
wa-anta l-yawma awʿaẓu minka ḥayyā[25]

Your life contained admonitions for me, but today you exhort more eloquently than you did while alive.

Section *E* too opens with an ambiguous statement (verse 28):

wa-laysat kal-ināthi wa-lā l-lawātī
tuʿaddu lahā l-qubūru mina l-ḥijāli

She was not like [*other*] *women; not like those for whom the grave is considered a curtained canopy.*

This is a slightly opaque line, perhaps prompted by the transition it provides to the description of the funeral:

29 wa-lā man fī janāzatihā tijārun
yakūnu wadāʿuhā nafḍa n-niʿāli
mashā l-umarāʾu ḥawlayhā ḥufātan . . .

Nor like one whose bier is followed by shopkeepers who say farewell by shaking the dust off their shoes. / Emirs walked barefoot around her bier . . .

We hardly notice how good the transition is, because by now we expect *ḥijāl*, the bridal canopy or alcove, to be picked up by something like *janāza*, "bier." The commentators take line twenty-eight to be a kind of variation on line ten. Yāzijī writes: "That is to say, she was a person of chastity and modest concealment (*tasattur*), unlike other women for whom the grave is considered a means of concealment."[26]

[25] *Kitāb al-aghānī*, III, 147. [26] *ʿArf*, II, 23.

This is Wāḥidī's view also.[27] The thing to observe is that *tu'addu lahā l-qubūru mina l-ḥijāli,* "the grave is considered a curtained canopy for them," is an inversion of *madfūnun qabla t-turbi ṣawnan,* "one who had been buried in chastity before she descended into the dust": chastity a kind of burial; being buried a kind of chastity. A similar inversion is at work in line thirty-seven:

wa-kam 'aynin muqabbalati n-nawāḥī
kaḥīlun bil-janādili war-rimāli

How many an eye whose borders were kissed all about
now wears mascara of stone and sand!

where "wears mascara of stone and sand" is the structural inverse of *mukaffan bil-jamāl,* "a person shrouded in beauty": the cosmetic of the grave and the winding sheet of loveliness. These variations are functional. The more they make us sense that metaphors of this kind move back and forth between life and death, easily and evenly as sinister pendulums, the more they blur the comforting boundary line between the two states. All of which has an odd effect on the final praise of Sayfaddawla:

41 wa-ḥālātu z-zamāni 'alayka shattā
wa-ḥāluka wāḥidun fī kulli ḥāli

The circumstances that affect you change with time, but
your condition is one and the same under all
circumstances.

Al-Mutanabbī's elegy coheres because it tests the possibilities of a single relation, the metaphorical tie between the

[27] *Dīwān Abī ṭ-Ṭayyib,* 392.

words of love and death. The availability of terms tagged by convention as belonging to the *ghazal* tradition enables the poet to do this very clearly. That the relation in question happens to be an ambivalence is an accidental property of the example I have chosen, but the technique of ringing the permutations of a single relation is common to many poems.

The Construction of Tales

six

An Allegory from the *Arabian Nights*: The City of Brass

Mais les bijoux perdus de l'antique Palmyre,
Les métaux inconnus, les perles de la mer,
Par votre main montés, ne pourraient pas suffire
A ce beau diadème éblouissant et clair;

Car il ne sera fait que de pure lumière,
Puisée au foyer saint des rayons primitifs,
Et dont les yeux mortels, dans leur splendeur entière,
Ne sont que des miroirs obscurcis et plaintifs!

—*Baudelaire, Bénédiction*

Gloomiest of travelogues, the tale of the City of Brass engages our attention in puzzling ways. Through its maze of episodes, conventional pessimism and the old cry *ubi sunt* are staged, sensed, and at last transcended. I am attempting a few remarks here on the nature and fascination of this maze, hoping to demonstrate its coherence and to show the source of its power.[1]

[1] I am using the Macnaghten text, *The Alif Laila* (Calcutta, 1839-1842), III, 83-115. In some places the Habicht-Fleischer edition, *Tausend und Eine Nacht* (Breslau, 1825-1843), VI, 343-401, is more complete, notably in the episode of the hill, where the Calcutta text promises seven tablets but fails to deliver all of them. Macnaghten's version shows not only more polish but also a sharper sense for dramatic detail. Habicht, for instance, lacks the striking observations about the ladder or the palace halls in the City of Brass. The queen's name

The story is an account of an archaeological expedition that consists of two parts: one planned and one fortuitous. In the opening scene, the caliph 'Abdalmalik ibn Marwān and his courtiers are seen discussing legends of the past. The talk turns on King Solomon's dominion over the jinn, and on the still extant brass bottles in which he imprisoned the refractory ones. The caliph is overwhelmed by curiosity, and at once an expedition is organized to the country in the far west where such bottles may be found. The project is successful, for, in spite of losing their way in the desert, the explorers manage to reach their destination and return to Damascus with several exhibits. Of the two leaders, Ṭālib ibn Sahl falls victim to his greed in the City of Brass, and the emir Mūsā, his task done, retires to a life of piety in Jerusalem. The hub of the tale is the visit to the City of Brass. It comes about when the party strays from the direct road, and its description is simply inserted in the larger narrative. This is not, however, an instance of the usual technique of employing a frame story to bring together many stories and hold the audience's attention by tying the parts into one. In our tale, the planned and the fortuitous are linked in a number of ways, and the links are among our first clues for understanding the storyteller's overall plan.

The explorers go off on a search after flotsam that has not yet gone under in time, and that, although it is flotsam, is a

---

is, I think, correct in Habicht's text and garbled in Macnaghten's, cf. p. 153 below. In any case, the differences between the two versions are not essential to the interpretation I am suggesting. Translators (Burton, Littmann, etc.) have generally followed Macnaghten and used Habicht to fill in lacunae.

The *City of Brass* is discussed at some length in M. I. Gerhardt, *The Art of Story-Telling* (Leiden, 1963), 195-235, where valuable historical data may be found. Gerhardt and I are at complete variance in our evaluations of structure, cohesion, and meaning in the story.

reminder of Solomon's glory. But already in the initial account of the brass bottles we come upon an ironic note. It is told that when one of the Solomonic seals is broken and a demon released, he gives a loud cry of repentance—prudently, for "the notion that Solomon is alive enters his mind."[2] The ambivalence of the jinn's cry will return to haunt the listener as the story progresses.

After a whole year's journey, the expeditionary party and their guide, a wise and pious shaykh, suddenly find that they are lost in the desert. This happens in the morning, and as they have nothing better to do they push on. By the time of midday prayer they come upon an imposing black castle, which the shaykh can identify. They are on an alternate road that leads from the black castle to the City of Brass, and then to the country of the bottles. It is curious that the narrator pays no attention at all to the travelers' plight, dramatic as their straying in the desert might be. He merely makes sure of providing a displacement with a jolt; descriptions do not concern him here. After a year on the road our explorers are snatched up and set on their way to the perverted time of the City, where past and present are confused by varied dissimulations.

The black castle is a kind of ghost town. There is no one about, and only inscriptions are there to tell the story of a vanished potentate's futile—and in the end ludicrous—efforts to resist mortality. M. Gerhardt sees the black castle as a prefiguration of the City of Brass, but she feels that "nothing happens in or because of it . . . and the whole episode serves no other purpose than to create a repository for the homilies given in the inscriptions."[3] I think that this instance of prefiguration is actually of great structural importance, all the more so because it is not the only one in the tale. With each antici-

[2] Macnaghten, 85.

[3] Gerhardt, *Art*, 207.

pated event, we are made aware of having been drawn towards it all along, and we sense that there is a kind of law to the direction taken by our ostensibly erratic divagations.[4] The relation between the castle and the City of Brass is such that we seem lured into a dream. The first episode is in a way realistic, while in the second the implicit menace of the first is given body to create a nightmare—a nightmare thus somehow born of our own minds.

On leaving the black castle, the travelers come upon a piece of magical engineering: the figure of a horseman cast in brass, which will swivel around at the touch of a hand and indicate the direction towards the City of Brass. This machine is not in itself evil, but it is ominous, as are other robots in the *Nights,* such as the uncanny boatman in the "Third Qalandar's Tale," or the horse in "The Ebony Horse." Magic and illusionist sculpture will both have a role in the City of Brass, as parts of an ironic setting.

Continuing their passage through the desert, the explorers find a column of black stone in which a demon is wedged. He tells a curious tale, and it appears that he was punished in this fashion by Solomon whom out of pride and folly he attempted to challenge. We are now explicitly brought back to the Solomonic motif of the apparent frame story. Apparent, because in fact the entire tale is very much of one piece; for in the central episode of the City of Brass the audience must recognize a series of allusions to Solomon, and the whole journey is calculated to stand out against the Solomonic *exemplum.*

[4] The *Faerie Queene* offers a good parallel. Guyon's progress through Phaedria's Island to Acrasia's Bower works this way, and so does Britomart's from Malecasta's pictures to Busirane's. Prefigurations give direction to our explorers' travels, and the same kind of thing happens to Spenser's protagonists on their rarely differentiated plain. The resulting feeling is described in Spenser's own line: "For who can shun the chance that destiny doth ordaine" (*FQ* III:i:37).

The exemplum has two sides. First: Solomon is an instance of mortal magnificence. The demon episode conjures up the pageantry of power from the Koran, recalling the jinn and the birds that served in the king's army, and mentioning his command of the wind. In the geographer Ibn al-Faqīh's version of the City of Brass legend, one of the inscriptions found on the city walls reads: "If any creature could attain eternal life, Solomon the son of David would have attained it."[5] It is as if the *Arabian Nights* had dropped this sentence in order to dramatize it instead.

Second: there is a darker aspect—Solomon's fall from grace and power. It is a temporary lapse according to the main line of Islamic tradition; the rabbinic opinions are more varied and more pessimistic.[6] In his *Stories of the Prophets*, Tha'labī tells us that Solomon possessed extraordinary powers by virtue of a ring that, in punishment for an act of idolatry committed under his roof, he once lost to a demon for a period of forty days.[7] During that time, the demon Ṣakhr imper-

[5] Ibn al-Faqīh al-Hamadhānī, *Compendium libri Kitab al-boldan*, ed. de Goeje (Leiden, 1885), 90. Quoted in Gerhardt, *Art,* 219-21.

[6] Cf. *Gittin*, 68b. It is debated whether Solomon was king and then commoner, or king, commoner and king again. Rashi, *ad loc.*, explains that only rule over the spirit world is meant. For the flawed figure of Solomon, cf. *Pesiqta Rabbati* 6:4, to the effect that Solomon would be one of the kings without a share in the world to come had he not built the Temple. An early example of the motif of Solomon's decline can be found near the end of the *Testament of Solomon*, transl. F. C. Conybeare, *Jewish Quarterly Review*, XI (1899), 45: "my spirit was darkened, and I became the sport of idols and demons." For a more far-flung instance, cf. Lidzbarski, *Ginza-Der Schatz oder das grosse Buch der Mandäer* (Göttingen, 1925), 28 and 46. In the Islamic version, Solomon does very well after recovering his ring, but a shadow remains. Cf. 'Aṭṭār's reminder that Solomon entered Paradise five hundred years later than the other prophets because of his ring of power, *Manṭiq aṭ-ṭayr*, ed. Gowharin (Tehran, 1964), 51.

[7] Tha'labī, *Qiṣaṣ al-anbiyā'* (Būlāq, 1869), 253-56. The story is at times questioned, e.g., Zamakhsharī, *Kashshāf*, to *wa-la-qad fatannā Sulay-*

sonates the king, who, driven from his house and made unrecognizable, becomes a fugitive. The story of this demonic fraud has provided medieval Koran commentators with one of the standard interpretations of the unclear, somber verse (38:34): *wa-la-qad fatannā Sulaymāna wa-alqaynā 'alā kursīyihi jasadan thumma anāba*, "We allowed Solomon to be seduced by temptation, and we cast a body upon his seat. Then he repented."

It is an important clue for understanding the entire tale that the demon in the rock is a close variation on Ṣakhr in the legend of the ring, and that his story is an unmistakable allusion to the demonic impersonation of Solomon. The *Arabian Nights* demon is punished because he aided and abetted a king who refused Solomon his daughter, and whose island realm Solomon then invaded. These events correspond to the exposition in the legend of the ring, where Solomon finally obtains the princess—to his grief, because it is the same princess' idolatry that later brings divine punishment upon him. Our demon is locked in a vise of stone; so is, in the legend, the impostor Ṣakhr at the end of his forty days' rule.[8] In the legend, Ṣakhr and his rock are thrown into the sea; this obviously could not be paralleled if the demon was to be a speaking character in the tale of the City of Brass.

The allusion to the outcast Solomon and to the deceptive body on the throne plays a number of essential roles. First:

---

māna (IV, 94 in the Beirut, 1947 ed.). Zamakhsharī actually implies that it was in some way Solomon's idea to have an image of the girl's father made (vs. Tha'labī, where the girl asks for the image that she then secretly worships), but he still finds it difficult to accept the whole affair as moral justification for Solomon's punishment. There are of course other available explanations for the verse. Some commentators have no interest at all in the moral reasons for Solomon's fall, cf. Qummī, *ad loc.* (II, 236-37 in the Najaf ed.).

[8] In the quoted passage by Qummī, several rebellious demons are locked into rocks, and several into bottles after this incident.

it strengthens the fabric of the tale because it is again a prefiguration; for in the City of Brass proper, various deceptive bodies (culminating in a body on a throne) will be the chief motifs. Second: as we shall see, the legend of Ṣakhr and Solomon is important because allegorical interpretations of it abounded in the Middle Ages. Third: the allusion is important *qua* allusion, because other implicit references to the Solomon material will follow, until in the end the story will appear not only as an allegory but also as a practical exercise in allusive reading.

When the emir Mūsā and his party finally come to the walls of the City of Brass and find no means of access, they climb up a hill that overlooks the enclosure. At the top, various tablets warn of the mutable nature of sublunary things, as well they might; for from the hill one looks down into the empty streets of the City. When the emir descends, he has seen the world for what it is worth.[9] Yet his education is not over. In the City of Brass knowledge through direct experience supplants received wisdom about mortality. From the hilltop Mūsā can see vacant streets and weeds growing in them, but he must pass through the gate before he comes across the bodies that are there.

The walls around the City are too high to measure, but when a ladder is made by estimate it fits exactly: not an inch too high or low. The City comes to meet its visitors.

Seductive girls beckon to those who scale the walls, but they are airy marionettes worked by magic, and a bait for the naive. The men, deceived by their charm, laugh and clap their hands in delight, then throw themselves down from the battlements and are immediately crushed. Fortunately the pious shaykh who guides the expedition sees through the trick: "All this is no doubt an enchantment and a trap devised

[9] Macnaghten, 101: *wa-qad ṣuwwira d-dunyā bayna ʿaynayh.* The phrase is missing in Habicht.

by the inhabitants of this town to keep off all those who might reconnoiter from above and then try to enter."[10] The girls are a product of human dissimulation. They are not there to protect the dead, but rather, left over from the City's lifetime, they are automata that go on functioning after their engineers have perished. The death-dealing mirage has been inherited by death itself: if during the life of the City this illusory life was a dissimulation to protect real life, it has now become dissimulation *per se*. The only life within the City walls is now of a fraudulent and essentially destructive kind.

At last the shaykh opens the gates from within, and a group of men enter the City of Brass. On their way to the palace, they must pass through the bazaar where the merchants' dead bodies are still sitting behind their wares, looking literally as if merely asleep. It is a hideous limbo.[11] Dying is here made perpetual, although death in action is nothing but apparitions and appearances. The inhabitants who created the apparitions are now themselves reduced to appearances. The irony is complete when Mūsā and his companions finally stand in front of the queen whom the emir takes to be alive. Ṭālib (or, in the Breslau version, the shaykh) enlightens him: "She is only a cunningly made simulacrum. Her eyeballs were removed after death, quicksilver was put under them, then they were reinserted. . . ."[12] The eyes blink and the eye-lashes move—more deceitful engineering. We realize that this manner of art was gently anticipated in the figurines of birds and beasts, found in previous rooms, which had bodies of gold and silver and whose eyes were rubies and pearls. "It

[10] Macnaghten, 103.

[11] It is interesting to contrast this motif with the belief that it is the bodies of the just that remain uncorrupted. For examples from midrash and *ḥadīth*, cf. R. Mach, *Der Zaddik in Talmud und Midrasch* (Leiden, 1957), 169.

[12] Macnaghten, 109; Habicht, 392-93.

was perplexing to look at them"—*yataḥayyaru kullu man ra'āhā*. The same verb describes the emotion aroused by the queen's body: *ta'ajjaba ghāyata l-'ajabi min jamālihā wa-taḥayyara min ḥusnihā wa-ḥumrati khaddayhā*, "he was amazed at her beauty, and confused by her charm and by the red in her cheeks."[13]

Impersonations, mirages, lifelike death. The motif that keeps obtruding is delusion-and-deceit, the *engaño* theme of the Spanish theatre or of the enchanted bowers of Renaissance epics. The travelers experience that death can look very much like life; after the princess with quicksilver under the eyes, we all blink for a while to make sure.

The City of Brass is tied to the Solomon legend in various ways, although Solomon's name seems to remain deliberately unmentioned. First of all, the audience will have been expected to know other versions of the tale, in which Solomon was the city's builder.[14] Second, one of the illusions—the motif of the floor glazed to look like water—is familiar from the story of Solomon and the Queen of Sheba (Koran 27:44).[15] Third, the dead princess bears the name Tadmura, and legend ascribes the building of Tadmur to Solomon.[16] Finally, with the story of Solomon and the jinn in the back-

[13] Macnaghten, 108. [14] Cf. Gerhardt, *Art*, 216-21.

[15] This motif is missing in Habicht's text.

[16] Gerhardt, *Art*, 205, is mistaken in considering the name arbitrary. For Solomon as the builder of Tadmur, cf. Yāqūt, *Mu'jam al-buldān*, *ad loc.* Yāqūt's quote from Nābigha Dhubyānī is 1:21-23 in Derenbourg's Paris 1869 edition of the dīwān. Islamic lands may have been acquainted with versions of the Solomon legend in which rule over Tadmur is one of the stages in the shrinking of the king's power. Cf. *Aggadat shir ha-shirim* 3:33-34, ed. Schechter, *JQR*, VII (1895), 150. Referred to in L. Ginzberg, *The Legends of the Jews* (Philadelphia, 1936), VI, 301.

The name Tadmura is also important for the provenience of the lifelike queen motif, cf. p. 161 below.

ground, the Muslim audience will hardly fail to recall Koran 34:14 upon hearing of deceptively lifelike corpses: *fa-lammā qaḍaynā ʿalayhi l-mawta mā dallahum ʿalā mawtihi illā dābbatu l-arḍi ta'ḵulu minsa'atahu* . . . , "and when We decreed his death, the only thing that made them [the jinn] realize that he was dead was a creeping thing of the earth that gnawed through his staff. . . ."

We must stop here a moment to consider what kind of death we saw in the City of Brass. How did the inhabitants perish? The queen's tablet explains that a famine had set in and everyone starved when gold could no longer buy food. As Gerhardt remarks, "viewed realistically, it is absurd: a population dying of hunger would not lay itself out as tidily, even pompously, as is described here. . . ." She suggests that the explanation may be a late, rationalizing addition, provided, together with other rhetorical matter in the inscriptions, by a "prolix man of letters."[17] But it is possible to see the question in a different light, and consider Macnaghten's text an intellectually and artistically respectable whole.

The explanation on the tablet is absurd, and it is meant to be that when realistically viewed. After all, the inscriptions warn us several times to "set aside provisions," and in those phrases the word *zād* must denote other provisions than bread and meat.[18] Its Islamic source is the one Koranic occurrence of the word (2:197): *wa-mā tafʿalū min ḵhayrin yaʿlamhu l-lāhu wa-tazawwadū fa-inna ḵhayra z-zādi t-taqwā,* "God knows of the good deeds you do. Store up provisions; for the best of provisions is the fear of God."[19] Our reading of the story must determine whether we take the *zād* mentioned in the City of Brass to mean piety, or rather food for thought: provisions for the mystic or gnostic traveler. At any

[17] Gerhardt, *Art,* 205.

[18] Macnaghten, 111, for instance.

[19] The idea of spiritual provisions is not, of course, limited to Islam. Cf. Mach, *Zaddik,* 190-94.

rate, here the journey in the tale becomes a spiritual one; the happenings in it ripen into metaphor and the tableaux into allegory. It is, so to speak, a *qūt al-qulūb*, "food for the heart," that is meant by *min 'adami l-qūti mātū*, "they died for lack of food."[20] In the City of Brass life is reduced to a kind of taxidermy because it is a place of spiritual starvation. It is not unrelated that elsewhere in the *Nights* magic tends to appear as a mode of power in its utmost capriciousness, but here it is a mode of futility, a misdirected effort at transcending the limits of humanity.

That the City of Brass is meant to be allegorical becomes even clearer upon the party's subsequent arrival at Karkar, where the coveted bottles are found. Here a light shines over the face of the earth on the night before Friday, and the natives are Muslims who learned their religion from Khiḍr, the divine intermediary and prototype of the esoteric knower, *'ārif*. After the black walls—and for that matter the towers that seemed of fire—that guarded the City of Brass, Karkar offers a complete contrast. The religion of Khiḍr is the alternative to spiritual famine. There is a curious touch: the visitors are given to eat the meat of fish in human shape. This is illusion with fangs drawn; here no one mistakes the outer form for the human being.[21]

It seems to me that on the basis of the queen's tablet we can exclude a purely ethical interpretation of the allegory. It is stressed there that the queen was a good and just ruler, unlike the self-centered author of the black castle inscriptions. Khiḍr and the light of Karkar suggest that *zād* is meant to have esoteric connotations.[22]

[20] Macnaghten, 105.

[21] For mystical initiation by Khiḍr, cf. L. Massignon, *Essai sur les origines du lexique technique de la mystique musulmane* (Paris, 1954), 131-32.

[22] By itself, the death-in-life motif occurs in ethical contexts; cf. the

At last the travelers return to Damascus. Of the things brought back, the jinn are released, the human-looking fish die of the heat, and the treasures are distributed among the Muslims.

We can now turn again to the question of coherence in the story. It seems to me that the attentive listener will see the sequence of ostensibly adventitious events united and made meaningful in two essential ways: (1) by the prefigurations through which the ultimate ironic experience of the City of Brass draws the voyagers towards itself, from "the notion that Solomon is alive enters his mind," through the black castle and the demon's allusion to the body on Solomon's throne, to Mūsā's perplexity before the dead queen; and (2) by the implicit presence of the Solomonic exemplum in passages that

---

saying attributed to Shaqīq ibn Ibrāhīm in Sulamī, *Kitāb ṭabaqāt aṣ-ṣūfīya*, ed. J. Pedersen (Leiden, 1960), 59: "God has made those who obey Him live in their death, and He has made those who rebel against Him dead during their lives." Esoteric uses of the motif are not particularly rare. For the story of the prince who mistakes a corpse for his bride, see p. 162 below. The Ismāʿīlī *Haft Bāb* describes the state of those who have missed the right path as "nonexistence dissembling existence," *nīstī-yi hastmānī*, cf. Abū Isḥāq Quhistānī, *Haft Bāb*, ed. and transl. W. Ivanow (Bombay, 1959), 49.

In an allegorical exegesis that is of some interest for unraveling our story, the same book equates pure food with an interpretation (*ta'wīl*) of the Koran that is free of confusions caused by literal understanding, *ẓāhir* (p. 56, to verse 4:160). Ibn 'Arabī's *Tafsīr* interprets the *ṭayyibāt* of 4:160 as divine manifestations.

In Habicht's Karkar, a column of light rises from the sea on the night before Friday, and a man walks on the water, reciting a creed formula. These two motifs are definitely mystical (or theosophic). They are linked in one passage, for example, in the *Kitāb al-mashāriʿ wal-muṭāraḥāt*, cf. Shihāb ad-Dīn Yaḥyā s-Suhrawardī, *Opera Metaphysica et Mystica*, ed. H. Corbin (Istanbul, 1945), I, 505, and the commentary to *'amūd aṣ-ṣubḥ* in the *Kitāb at-talwīḥāt*, p. 108 in the same volume.

seem to stand in an accidental relation to the "frame story." It may be added here that the explicitly Solomonic sections are more or less symmetrically placed, the demon episode coming between the black castle and the City of Brass.

With its insistence on false appearances, the tale acts out the idea of the world as mirage, which one of the homilies speaks about, and it forces us to experience the concern about provisions that is reiterated in the inscriptions. It is an error to think that the tale is somehow draped around the properly homiletic passages in it and exists for their sake, but it is quite as wrong to regard them as cumbersome adjuncts devised by a pedantic litterateur. The reading of the tablets and the emir's ritualistic crying in response[23] are performative acts through which the story reaffirms, and participates in, a collective mood. At the same time, however, the allegory invites the audience to go beyond a trivial understanding of the homilies. For people who have seen (or would see) Karkar, going on a journey—the *irtiḥāl* of the homilies—will come to stand for other voyages besides that of death.[24]

But the true homiletic effect of the story springs from its structure, and particularly from the structural harmony between the line followed by Mūsā's journey on the one hand, and the affair of Solomon and the jinn on the other. If the story of the City of Brass was meant to be interpreted, one of the questions to be asked must be why the imprisoned jinn

[23] Cf. the article *bakkā'*, by F. Meier, in the second edition of the *Encyclopaedia of Islam.*

[24] I do not mean that the world-renouncing aspect is invalidated, but that it is kept as a first level, while the story implies that one must pass beyond it. To see the world of experience as a sort of shell or model, and to realize that it is to the intelligible world as darkness is to light is a "first ascent," *al-mi'rāj al-awwal*, for the man starting out towards the divine presence, cf. Ghazālī, *Mishkāt al-anwār* (Cairo, 1964), 50.

are found at Karkar, the place of light. In a none-too-clear passage, Khiḍr and the imprisoned jinn are linked in Ibn al-Faqīh's version of the legend too,[25] but the *Arabian Nights* story stresses the opposition between the City and Karkar to an extent that invites—and expects—further probing. Islamic mystical literature, not unexpectedly, abounds in references to Solomon and the demons, and a few of these will answer our question. In the "Tale of the Occidental Exile," by Suhrawardī of Aleppo, the obedient jinn who served Solomon appear together with the Koranic fountain of molten brass that they fire up and fashion into a wall.[26] The Persian commentary equates the jinn with the powers of imagination and thought, the fountain with mystical wisdom, and the wall with protection against the Gog and Magog of worldliness. By a similar logic, in Ibn 'Arabī's commentary to Koran 34:12 (*wa-man yazigh minhum*, etc.), the rebellious jinn stand for the inclination towards the allurements of sensual drives (*nafs*).[27] For our story, the demon episode (with its allusion to the legend of Solomon's ring and his forty days' exile) turns out to be crucial in the light of examples like the following two from 'Aṭṭār: *dīv-rā vaqtī k̠e dar zindān k̠unī—bā Sulaymān qaṣd-i shādurvān k̠unī*, "If you bind the demon, you will set out for the royal pavilion with Solomon" and *az ān bar mulk̠-i k̠hvīshat nīst farmān—k̠e dīvat hast bar jā-yi Sulaymān*, "You have no command over your self's kingdom, for in your case the demon is in the place of Solomon."[28]

[25] *K. al-buldān*, 91.

[26] Cf. *Qiṣṣat al-ghurba al-gharbīya*, in *Oeuvres philosophiques et mystiques de Shihabaddin Yahya Sohrawardi* [*Opera Metaphysica et Mystica*, II], ed. H. Corbin (Tehran, 1952), 285.

[27] II, 303-05 in the Beirut, 1968 edition.

[28] *Manṭiq aṭ-ṭayr* 35 (line 612), and *Ilāhīnāme*, ed. H. Ritter (Istanbul, 1940), 289 (line 12). Reference to the second passage in H. Ritter, *Das Meer der Seele* (Leiden, 1955), 625.

Finally, in Ibn 'Arabī's multilayered commentary to *wa-la-qad fatannā Sulaymāna,* etc., Solomon's changed appearance after the loss of the ring means, among other things, a distortion of original luminousness.[29] In view of these examples, we can say that the explicit statement on rebellious demons (that they are imprisoned in Karkar) and the allusion to the demon who once had the upper hand over Solomon form a neat bundle if, and only if, the story is read allegorically.

In the Islamic version of the legend of the ring, it is after the ring is recovered that Solomon asks for and receives a power unique in the world. Mūsā's journey follows a similar sequence. The deceptive bodies in the City of Brass, as mementoes of spiritual starvation, parallel the demonic impersonation of Solomon and the spiritual loss of the true self. The party's arrival at Karkar corresponds to recovering the ring and casting out the usurper and illusionist. Obviously, both story lines can be interpreted in a number of ways, whether as examples of pride and fall, or as gnostic tales of the soul's exile and return. The pattern of symbolism could accommodate the Ghazālī of the *Mishkāt al-anwār* as well as it would suit an Ismā'īlī, Suhrawardī, or 'Aṭṭār. What matters is that the two sets of motifs are composed, not patched together.

Whatever the precise intent of the allegory, the allusive technique used in the story provides the reader with an exercise in interpretation. The journey invites a symbolic reading, *ta'wīl*, and the Solomon motif a parallel reading, *taṭbīq*.[30] The emphasis on interpretation would still fit many directions of thought, and the denotations of terms that may have been used technically—such as *ma'ād*, "return," "the life to come,"

[29] II, 356 in the Beirut, 1968 edition.

[30] Cf. I. Goldziher, *Die Richtungen der islamischen Koranauslegung* (repr. Leiden, 1952), 244.

etc., for example—must depend on the storyteller's doctrine, if indeed he held an exact one.[31] Certain motifs, such as the glazed floor, are likely to have been inserted with a *ta'wīl* in mind, or perhaps simply as inducements to interpretation.[32]

[31] Cf. *ma'ād* in *Rasā'il Ikhwān aṣ-ṣafā'* (Beirut, 1957), IV, 50; *Haft Bāb*, 47; and Daylamī, *Bayān madhhab al-bāṭinīya wa-buṭlānih*, ed. Strothmann (Istanbul, 1939), 37 and 78.

[32] For the glazed floor, cf. Ibn 'Arabī's *Tafsīr*, II, 205, or Ḍiyā' ad-Dīn Ismā'īl ibn Hibatallāh al-Ismā'īlī s-Sulaymānī, *Mizāj at-tasnīm*, ed. Strothmann as *Ismailitischer Koran-Kommentar* (Göttingen, 1944; Abh. Ak. Wiss. Gött., Phil.-Hist. Kl., Dritte Folge, Nr. 31), 334.

The death of Ṭālib could be interpreted in various ways. Politically, for Ṭālib wants to earn the Umayyad caliph's favor by making him a gift of the queen's jewels. Esoterically, if we take the *amāna*, "trust," which Ṭālib breaks as an allusion to Koran 33:72. For *amāna* = *ma'rifa*, "gnosis," cf. Fakhr ad-Dīn ar-Rāzī, *At-tafsīr al-kabīr*, *ad loc.* Admittedly, it is an old device of plots that only one of two bold heroes escapes unscathed; in this sense Ṭālib is of the line of Enkidu and Pirithous.

It is perhaps more than an accident that the queen is found in the seventh room of the palace, although the author does not mention the number.

Finally, although the City of Brass is traditionally placed in North Africa—which makes arguments about geographical symbolism unsafe—it is tempting to think that the author is telling us something by giving the name Tadmura (or keeping it if there is a separate prototype for her figure) to a Maghribine princess from beyond the desert of Qayrawān, even though the name is clearly linked to Palmyra. Qayrawān, according to the *Burhān-i Qāṭi'*, is among other things a term for the edges of the world; one is tempted to think of Alexander's search for the spring of life in the land of darkness. Quite specifically, in Suhrawardī's *Qiṣṣat al-ghurba al-gharbīya*, 277, Qayrawān is *al-qarya aẓ-ẓālim ahluhā*, "the town of iniquitous inhabitants" (Koran 4:75), where the protagonist is held in captivity. The place is explained by the commentator: *Qayrawān ya'nī 'ālam va bi-ẓālim 'ālamīyān khvāste and*, "Qayrawan means the world, and the people of the world are meant by 'the iniquitous.'" One wonders whether there is any implication that one *must* pass through the dark walls of the City of Brass

Gerhardt lists a number of other versions of the City of Brass legend in Arabic.[33] Most interesting in regard to prototypes is the passage from Ibn al-Faqīh al-Hamadhānī, which mentions Solomon, Khiḍr, and brass creatures emerging from brass bottles. It is very striking that in this version Mūsā's men are afraid of losing their provisions to the brass men, who are demons.[34] As I have said, Ibn al-Faqīh (or the compendium of his work) leaves many aspects of the anecdote obscure. The role of Khiḍr, for instance, is quite incomprehensible. Our author obviously used a version like Ibn al-Faqīh's, but, as far as one can tell, his use of the motifs he found is quite original.

None of the versions includes the lifelike corpse of the queen, which, however, probably has a prototype in a separate quasi-historical narrative about Palmyra. In the article *Tadmur*, Yāqūt's geographical dictionary relates that the unconsumed body of a long-dead princess was found when the walls of Palmyra were broken through. In that instance the corpse was a malevolent one, with a curse that was duly fulfilled. Ṭālib (who is killed by a robot when he tries to rob the dead queen of her jewels) may have been sacrificed to propitiate this proto-queen for the abrogation of her curse in the *Arabian Nights* story. It may also be to our purpose that, as

before one may come to the Karkar of the mind. Was the route originally planned at all possible? Corbin interprets the *barzakh* in Avicenna's *Risālat Ḥayy ibn Yaqẓān* as such a necessary passage through the dark, cf. *Avicenna and the Visionary Recital*, transl. W. Trask (New York, 1960), 142 and 159, but against that view cf. A.-M. Goichon, *Le récit de Ḥayy ibn Yaqẓān* (Paris, 1959), 86-90. The text of the passage in question is in *Traités mystiques d'Abou Alî al-Hosain b. Abdallah b. Sînâ*, ed. M. A. F. Mehren (Leiden, 1889), fasc. 1, p. 8 of the Arabic text.

33 Gerhardt, *Art*, 210-30.

34 Ibn al-Faqīh, *K. al-buldān*, 88-91.

the same article mentions, Tadmur was celebrated for some statues of girls that were perfectly preserved among the ruins.

Mistaking the dead for the living is not an uncommon motif. Its best-known example in Islamic literature is perhaps the anecdote of the prince who strays from his palace during his wedding feast and, drunk, spends the night in a cemetery, taking a corpse for his bride. The story is used as a gnostic parable of the soul's pre-existence and return from its terrestrial sojourn, in the forty-eighth epistle of the Sincere Brethren.[35]

It complicates the problem of prototypes to compare the version of the story in the Hebrew *Ma'asēh ha-n^e^mālāh,*[36] where Solomon himself comes to a desolate castle whose inhabitants died of famine. Even the inscribed counsels tally: *qaḥ l^e^ḵā ṣēdāh la-dereḵ,* "provide for the road," it reads over a lintel. In this castle, however, our cadavers are reduced to illusionist statuary inhabited by demons. There is no land of light; the midrash is essentially about the folly of pride and worldliness. It is possible that a common prototype of the "City of Brass" and the *Ma'asēh ha-n^e^mālāh* existed once, in which the motifs of famine (with properly disintegrated bodies) and of statues with moralistic inscriptions already appeared. Such statues may even have brought on the association of Tadmura.

In their epistle about themselves, the Sincere Brethren define certain stations through which the would-be initiate must

[35] IV, 162-64. The *Epistles of the Sincere Brethren* are a tenth-century compendium of science, philosophy, and religion, Ismā'īlī in politics and Neoplatonic-emanationist in metaphysics. The story also occurs in 'Aṭṭār's *Ilāhīnāme,* as pointed out by Ritter, *Meer,* 47. The basic motif is widespread. For a curious example from Europe, cf. C. Nodier, *Infernaliana* (Paris, 1966), 96-97.

[36] A. Jellinek, *Bet ha-Midrasch* (repr. Jerusalem, 1967), pt. V, 22-26. Referred to in Ginzberg, *Legends,* VI, 298.

pass. At the station that follows formal affirmation and precedes verification by the heart, *at-taṣdīq biḍ-ḍamīr,* matters of doctrine must be pictured in the mind by means of *amthāl,* "parables."[37] Such was the job our author chose when he took his legends and images and made them into provisions for the imagination.[38] The job, to be sure, did not diminish his delight in telling a tale to set our hair on end.

[37] IV, 58. I think that, considering the Sincere Brethren's predilection for allegorical tales, *amthāl* must mean "parables" or "allegories" here, and not "maxims," *gnōmai.* (The latter are a means of the rhetorical method of *taṣdīq* according to Averroes. Cf. H. A. Wolfson, "The Terms *Taṣawwur* and *Taṣdīq* in Arabic Philosophy and Their Greek, Latin and Hebrew Equivalents," *The Moslem World,* XXXIII [1943], 118.)

[38] The Iranian tradition of the Brazen Hold seems to have no direct bearing on our tale. The travelers' route is unlike the seven stages Isfandiyār must traverse. Sinbādh (*Siyāsatnāme,* 45) proclaimed that Abū Muslim, the Mahdī, and Mazdak were waiting to return together from a brazen fort, but our City is anything but Messianic. On the Iranian motif, cf. K. Czeglédy, "Bahrām Čōbīn and the Persian Apocalyptic Literature," *Acta Orientalia Acad. Sci. Hung.,* VIII (1958), 21-43. For the references to Isfandiyār and Bahrām Chūbīn, I am indebted to Prof. M. Dickson of Princeton.

seven

The Music of the Spheres: The Porter and the Three Ladies of Baghdad

1

If in the *City of Brass* ostensibly random events appear coherent when examined in the light of their references to a revealed moral order in the universe,[1] in the tale of *The Porter and the Three Ladies of Baghdad* there is a structural coherence that ultimately speaks for a morally random universe.[2] The two stories represent two poles of thought in the *Nights*, and both demonstrate that storytellers took up the moral interest upon which the Arabic poets of the later Middle Ages had turned their backs.

Since my discussion will focus on the relations among various details of the story, I must begin with a somewhat lengthy synopsis.

After making a delivery, a porter from the market manages to get himself invited to spend a few hours at the house of his

[1] It might be objected that a radical Ismāʿīlī reading of the tale would not have been concerned with a moral order. But in fact the radicalism of such readers would have lain in their belief that they were in possession of a knowledge that illuminated a higher morality, superseding the morality of the vulgar. It might also be objected that there were mystics who courted a whimsical God. No doubt, but the tale of the City of Brass is perhaps much too systematic to have been of any allegorical use to them.

[2] Macnaghten, I, 56-141; Habicht, I, 146-349.

customers, three mysterious young women who later turn out to be half-sisters. They drink, sing, and play seductive games. Day turns to night. There is a knocking at the door; three men arrive, dressed and shaven like wandering dervishes. Each of them is blind in one eye. They explain that they are strangers in Baghdad, ask for shelter, and are allowed in. Not long after this, the caliph Hārūn ar-Rashīd, who happens to be making an incognito tour of the city, hears enticing sounds of merrymaking issuing from the house, and wants to enter. He will not be dissuaded by his companion, the vizier; they knock, explain their presence by a story that is just peculiar enough to be credible, and are asked to join the party. Each new arrival is sternly warned, by word of mouth and by an inscription on the walls, to keep out of business that does not concern him or else run the risk of a bitter experience. At first all goes well.

Suddenly the hosts begin to do surprising things. Two black bitches are brought in. One of the girls proceeds to whip the dogs until she can go on no longer; then, sobbing, she hugs and kisses them. At last the dogs are led away. Now the second young woman asks the third for music. She complies and sings a number of melancholy love poems, until the second sister rends her clothes and falls down in a faint. Naked, her body shows the marks of a brutal flogging. When she comes to, new clothes are brought and the whole scene of singing, rending, and fainting is repeated twice more.

The guests' capacity for discretion is now exhausted. They cast their promise aside and demand an explanation for the odd events of the night. At a signal from the girls armed slaves appear, immobilize the imprudent questioners and make ready to slaughter them. Reciting an elegant love poem, the porter begs for mercy. Sure enough, the mistress of the house relents. She turns the situation around: the guests may go free, but not until they have told their several histories. The dervishes are all princes who suffered various misfortunes, and now their tales follow.

On a visit to his uncle's kingdom, the first prince is asked by his cousin for help in an unusual project. The cousin and a heavily veiled woman descend into a crypt, and the hero is requested to wall up the entrance and render it invisible. He does this so well that even he cannot find the place again. He returns to his father's kingdom, but in the meantime the father has been overthrown by his evil vizier. The vizier once lost an eye, hit by an arrow that the young prince had aimed at a bird; he has hated our hero ever since, and now exacts punishment in kind. Still unsatisfied, he orders the prince killed, but the executioner lets him go. The prince flees to his uncle's kingdom. The old man still mourns his son's disappearance; the prince tells him about the crypt; they go in search of the place and this time it lets itself be found. They break the seal, they enter, and in a vaulted room stocked with provisions, on a canopied bed, they find two charred bodies.

The old man immediately grasps what must have taken place. The prince's cousin and the cousin's own sister, who had long been in love, attempted to find safety and leisure in this catacomb, where the fire of divine retribution instead of the pleasanter flames of lust devoured them. The uncle is about to adopt the hero as his heir when a great din of arms is heard: the evil vizier's soldiers have invaded the city. The uncle is killed; the young man must flee for his life. He takes the road to Baghdad, where at the city gate he meets the second and third dervishes on the very night of their subsequent encounter with the three ladies.

The second prince's narrative opens with his journey to visit the king of India. En route he is attacked by bandits. He escapes but finds himself in a strange city where a kind tailor puts him up and gives him a woodcutter's ax to earn a living with. One day, while digging around a tree he has chosen to fell, the prince discovers the entrance to an underground palace. Inside he finds a girl of great beauty who explains that on her wedding night she was kidnapped by a demon and deposited in this hideaway, where he comes to sleep with her every tenth night. Should she need anything, she can summon him by touching the inscribed threshold. The lady invites the hero to keep her company at table and in bed until her next appointment with the demon, and the two spend their time quite agreeably until the prince, befuddled with wine and happiness, determines to take care of the kidnapper once and for all. He summons the demon, but sobers up soon enough when he arrives. The hero takes to his heels, but in his haste leaves shoes and ax behind. Chains, whipping, and torture fail to compel the lady to confess to the demon, but the telltale ax soon leads him to the tailor's place. The demon unceremoniously returns the prince to the cavern for a confrontation.

In the end, the ifrit chops his mistress into pieces but, not being entirely certain of the hero's guilt, merely changes him into a monkey, who then roams about until he comes to a seacoast, where he is picked up by a merchant ship. Fortunately, the monkey has retained the prince's intelligence, education, and elegant skills; his calligraphy comes to a king's attention and he is granted audience. The monkey makes a brilliant debut, and when the king's daughter, versed in the magical arts, recognizes him for an enchanted man, the king asks her to return the monkey to human shape so that our hero can become the king's vizier and the daughter's husband. She resolves to summon up the ifrit and fight him until the spell is broken. It is a long and desperate fight. The contestants take on various shapes; they fight under the ground and in the air. At last the girl changes into fire and manages to destroy the demon. A stray spark blinds the monkey in the right eye, but he does regain human form. The adventure ends badly. The magic fire called up by the princess will not now let her go: a few minutes after the end of the struggle a horrible spontaneous combustion reduces her to ashes. The prince must leave the country. He shaves his beard, puts on a dervish's robe, and takes the road to Baghdad.

The story of the third dervish-prince, 'Ajīb, begins with his shipwreck at the Adamant Mountain. The mariners are all killed, but 'Ajīb survives, being the one destined to tumble a magical brass rider from the top of the cliff into the waves and rid navigation of the statue's lethal magnetism. In a dream 'Ajīb is instructed what to do, and he is told that after the task is accomplished a brass oarsman will appear, to row him to familiar shores. Everything happens as foretold, but when near deliverance 'Ajīb cannot suppress a happy *Allāh akbar*—against which he was warned in the dream—and as soon as the name of God is uttered he finds himself thrown from the boat, which sinks. The young man is deposited on an island by a big wave, just in time to observe a great number of slaves carrying provisions from a ship into a subterranean apartment. At last a boy is led into the cave by an old man. The old man reappears alone; the entrance is covered up, and all but the boy re-embark and sail away.

'Ajīb immediately makes his way into the hiding place, where the boy explains that he was concealed there by his father because the astrologers had read in his horoscope that, at the age of fifteen, he would die at the hands of the man who toppled the brass rider from the Adamant Mountain. Within fifty days after the rider's fall the boy would be killed, but if he chanced to survive this period, the danger would be over. It is now ten days since the brass rider sank into the sea; there are forty more left.

'Ajīb is flabbergasted. Nothing could be further from him than the desire to kill this beautiful boy. He does not disclose his identity, but offers to keep the boy company and to serve him during his period of concealment. The two play checkers, talk, and become good friends. On the fortieth day the boy asks 'Ajīb for some melons. Jumping to oblige, 'Ajīb reaches for the knife kept on an upper shelf, stumbles, falls and stabs the boy. The old man and his slaves arrive; they find the child's body and leave lamenting. 'Ajīb manages to escape notice. After a month, during which the sea keeps ebbing, he can cross to dry land. His journey takes him to a castle plated in brass in which ten young men live, all blind in the right eye. They allow him in but warn him against inquiring about the reason for their state. A familiar motif: violent rituals of mourning after dinner arouse the visitor's curiosity, and he wants at any cost to know the story of the ten. Reluctantly, they let him find out for himself. They sew him into a sheepskin that the rokh bird carries up to a mountain top; there he cuts the skin open and walks to a palace, which he enters. Forty splendid girls receive him; together and singly they offer him the luxurious delights of their company. But on the first day of the new year the girls, all princesses, must leave for forty days to visit their parents. They leave the keys of the castle's hundred rooms with 'Ajīb, who should find adequate entertainment in the marvels that ninety-nine of them contain. Were he to enter the hundredth room, he would be forever parted from the girls. The doors open on ravishing gardens, refreshing meadows, prodigious treasures. On the fortieth day 'Ajīb cannot resist opening the hundredth door. There is a great black horse in the room; 'Ajīb mounts, and strikes the immobile horse with a whip. It then spreads powerful wings, flies through the air, and arriving at the palace of the ten throws its rider and strikes him in the face with its tail. 'Ajīb loses an eye. The palace only has room for the ten who are already there; 'Ajīb puts on a dervish's gear and makes his way to Baghdad.

The caliph and the vizier repeat the story that served them as a pretext for their visit. The guests are now allowed to leave the house. The next day Hārūn has the ladies and the dervishes summoned, and orders the three sisters to account for their actions of the previous night. The girl with the dogs is first to speak.

She has two sisters by the same father and mother, and two —the scarred girl and the third resident of the house—by the same father and a different mother. Her tale involves the first two. After the parents' death, the uterine sisters divide the three thousand dinars left by their mother; the narrator goes into the textile business and prospers; the two elder sisters marry husbands who impoverish and abandon them. The heroine takes them into her house and treats them well, but they have not learned from their experiences and marry again. Everything is repeated. Some time after the sisters' second retreat to her house, the young woman decides to go on a business trip. The sisters accompany her. On the high seas her ship strays off course and reaches land near a city whose inhabitants have all been turned to stone. After some strolling in the royal quarter, the lady comes upon a single live person: a young man who can satisfy her curiosity. The residents of the city, ruled by the young man's father, had been fire worshippers. One day a heavenly voice commanded them to forsake their heathen practices and worship God instead. All refused obstinately and all were turned to stone, except the prince, who had been receiving secret instruction in Islam. The lady proposes to the lonely survivor. He accepts, but to his misfortune: to see their successful sister happily engaged is too much for the twice-divorced women and they throw the fiancés overboard. The pious prince drowns at once, but the business lady reaches the shore. Here she rescues a serpent that is pursued by a dragon. The grateful serpent—who is in fact a Muslim demoness—determines to do the heroine a good turn. She fetches the wicked sisters and turns them into dogs, and then takes lady and dogs back to the house in Baghdad. There the demoness orders the lady to administer three hundred lashes to each animal night after night, failing which she too would be turned into a dog and shut up underground.

The scarred lady's story is less miraculous. She is lured by an old hag into a strange house where she meets a beautiful young man who proposes to marry her. She accepts; they draw up the marriage contract. His only condition is that she should never set eyes upon another man. The marriage is a happy one until the same old woman takes the heroine to the bazaar, where a young merchant refuses to sell her the cloth she picks out except at the price of a kiss on the cheek. The hag convinces the lady that the matter is of no great consequence; the lady complies and the merchant bites deep into her cheek. The husband is not taken in by his wife's version of the event. His slaves tie her up and set about cutting her in two. The old woman rushes in to plead for the lady's life. The husband foregoes putting her to death, but punishes her with a savage flogging, after which the slaves take the unconscious lady back to her old house. After she recovers she goes to see the husband's palace and finds the whole street in ruins. She goes to live with her half-sister—the first lady—and they are joined by their father's last daughter, the lady without a story.

All is now told. The caliph has the first lady summon the serpent-demoness, who materializes at once and upon Hārūn's bidding releases the spellbound dogs. She then announces that the scarred lady's husband was no other than al-Amīn, the heir-apparent. It is now Hārūn's turn to take center stage and do justice. He marries off the first lady and her once wicked sisters to the three one-eyed dervishes whom he appoints his chamberlains. He reinstates the marriage of his son al-Amīn with the flogged lady, and he himself marries the lady who had no story to tell.

The reader will immediately notice that the tale is a series of echoes and reflections. The design is at times obvious, at times half hidden in a tangle of details, but never lacking. My purpose is to examine the relation between the formal coherence of events in the story and the storyteller's evaluation of the moral coherence among the events he narrates. It could be argued that the structural properties of the tale, the neat and interesting relations among motifs and variations on motifs, are not unlike musical relations, and that the pleasure the audience derives from them is a musical pleasure. It could also be argued that periodicity is a storyteller's device for holding the audience's attention. You know that something is destined to happen again, but you also know that it will come in by a different door or even a window. Of course you are curious to see how an analogous result comes about through a different process, but you are not necessarily concerned with the good and the evil of it, or with the question whether or not the actors in the different episodes deserved the same fate.

Both lines of argument are unobjectionable, but they do not take care of the entire matter, because our story contains not only design but also a critique of design. It would be foolish of the critic to overlook that some writers consciously explore, or meditate on, such relations among events as often serve, without being made explicit, as underlying patterns of mythological thought. Compare Edgar to Edmund, *Lear*, v, iii, 172-73:

> The dark and vicious place where he thee got
> Cost him his eyes.

Our storyteller meditates on the very fact of evident design behind his events. "What a coincidence," the ladies exclaim, and go on to find out by a kind of gradual revelation that there is coincidence behind coincidence. Their exclamation is followed by the storyteller's implicit questionings of the patterns that make up the design. I will first discuss the patterns, and then the implicit critique.

2

The invariants in the dervishes' narratives are simple to summarize; they are obvious and they dominate the entire tale. One is apparent as soon as the three men cross the threshold: all three are blind in one eye. Then, as they begin to relate their experiences, we note that there is a set of invariants that occurs in each man's report. Each is a prince; each has been involved with a splendidly equipped underground hiding place; each has contributed in one way or another to the destruction of the occupants of these catacombs.

A storytelling technique is also shared by the three narratives, and it is a very striking one: within each of the three there is a duplication of some dominant motif.

In the first narrative there are two descents into the vault, and there are two instances of armed invasion, in which it is the prince's father and adoptive father who are successively killed. In the second narrative there are two ladies killed on account of the prince. In the third narrative the doubling is most blatant, and of a type that is familiar from all kinds of folklore: forty days are spent in the cave and forty days in the forty ladies' castle; there is a magic horse in each half; the brass boatman in the first part is followed by the brass walls of the castle in the second. (The ladies' tales too have some doubled elements, although the duplicate structure is not as strict as in the events related by the men. The first lady's wicked sisters are twice deserted by their husbands; the second lady's marriage and repudiation are both brought about by the same old woman.) It should be noted that the doublings in the dervishes' narratives represent a periodicity in time, while the other repeated invariants (blindness, etc.) represent a periodicity by juxtaposition. The two (which could be charted along two co-ordinates) complement one another and give an impression of a self-sufficient, orderly system.

There are other sets of complementary elements, which reinforce this impression. The person or persons found underground are voluntarily there in the first case, under constraint in the second, and in the third episode the boy is there voluntarily to avoid what is in fact the constraint of destiny. Furthermore, the three realms of *Arabian Nights* storytelling are all represented: the human in the first narrative, the human and demonic in the second, the human and the magical in the third. The two most intriguing instances of such complementary distribution have to do with the loss of the eye.

First: the relations among (1) the loss of one eye, (2) the descent into the vault, and (3) the doubling of certain motifs vary from episode to episode. In the first instance, the loss of an eye is not caused by the events underground, nor does it depend on the duplicate structure of the story. In the second, both relations are positive: the mutilation occurs as a result of what took place in the demon's hideaway, but it only comes about *via* the doubling. The third episode is paradoxical: there is no causal relation between cave and eye, but a very close formal one, since the eye is lost at the end of the second period of forty days.

Second: the hero's responsibility for the loss of one eye is not the same in each case. He is not held responsible (by himself or by the author) in the first episode: there was certainly no intention behind the shooting accident that deprived the malevolent vizier of an eye. ʿAjīb, in the third narrative, is fully responsible for his misfortune, and he acknowledges as much. The second dervish's case falls in the uncertain zone here: he was drunk when he first summoned the jinni and initiated the chain of catastrophes.

Before examining further the storyteller's use of these periodicities and complementary motifs, we must look at a third set of orders. These are the echoes (parallels or inversions) that form one-to-one links among the first two dervishes and ladies in a variety of ways. The third dervish's story does not fit in here, which is quite proper since the third lady has no story. Let me tabulate these relations, with *A* and *B* standing for the first two dervishes and *X* and Y for the ladies, (*p*) for a parallel and (*i*) for an inverse relation:

A/B (i)	*A*—uncle's sinful son burned to death (uncle also adoptive father)
	B—prospective father-in-law's good daughter burned to death
X/Y (i)	*X*—flogs hounds and then laments
	Y—laments and then reveals traces of having been flogged
A/X (i)	*A*—story dominated by motif of incest between siblings
	X—story dominated by attempted murder of a sibling
B/Y (p)	*B*—lady flogged by jealous demon
	Y—lady flogged by jealous husband
A/Y (p)	*A*—cannot find the tomb again
	Y—cannot find the husband's house again[3]

[3] This (*p*) is weak, since the house is in ruins but the site can be found. It is remarkable that not finding the tomb is simply a sign of divine interference. The tomb of a saintly sufi is unrecognizable in Abū Nuʿaym al-Iṣbahānī, *Ḥilya*, II, 84.

B/X (i) *B*—evil demon finds hero in souterrain
—evil demon turns hero into a beast
—hero indirectly causes death of girl who calls up the powers of fire (to fight the demon)
X—good demoness threatens to lock heroine in a subterranean prison if she fails to carry out certain instructions[4]
—good demoness turns villains into beasts
—heroine indirectly causes death of young man who has forsaken the powers of fire (abandoned worship of fire)

The story of the third dervish (who is in an anomalous position for lack of a lady counterpart) contains, within itself, a number of inverse relations. In the first part of his narrative 'Ajīb topples the magic horse; in the second part another magic horse throws 'Ajīb. At the end of the first sequence of forty days he commits manslaughter but remains unharmed; at the end of the second he commits a mere indiscretion but is mutilated.

3

To purely structural inquiry, the dervishes' narratives yield a meaning. I think that this meaning is not the entire meaning of the tale, but it undeniably plays a role—in something like a drama of meanings.

The clue is a very short parenthetical story that I did not include in the synopsis. It deals with clemency, and it is told by the second dervish in an attempt to mollify the jinni who is threatening to kill him. A good man is *thrown into a pit* by an envious man. The good man, while in the pit, overhears some demons who discuss a method for curing a possessed

[4] Habicht, I, 326. Not in Macnaghten.

princess. He manages to get out, heals the girl, and becomes her father's vizier. When he meets the envious villain again, he repays his enemy with kindness. If we take this seemingly extraneous piece into consideration—and its central position, in the middle of the second dervish's tale, lends it weight, just as the story of Ṣakhr is emphasized by its position in the *City of Brass*—we get a new picture of the invariant motifs, which can be presented in the form of a proportion: the relation between voluntary descent and physical vision is the inverse of the relation between involuntary descent and spiritual vision. In each case the descent is to a frontier of the underworld: the good man is thrown into the pit that he may die; the dervishes descend by their own will and meet liminal characters who either have fled life as it is normally lived or have been snatched from it, and who are destined to meet a violent death. In many mythological traditions the motif of mutilation signals persons who in some way mediate between life and death,[5] and at times (as in the case of Teiresias) the loss of physical sight goes with increased wisdom. In our story, however, half-blindness is merely a loss, a diminution occasioned by the wrong kind of mediation between life and death.

As we have seen, the different degrees of responsibility that the dervishes must bear for the loss of one eye form a complementary set, and we may now be very much tempted to agree that the variety of intention and guilt merely contributes to establishing the universality of the law stated by our proportion, and that the complementary aspect of responsibilities invites no more question than does the complementary distribution of hero's helpers—fish, bird, quadruped—in the Russian folktale.[6] But this will not quite do.

[5] Cf. C. Lévi-Strauss, *Mythologiques*, I (Paris, 1964), 61.

[6] Cf. V. Propp, *Morphology of the Folktale*, transl. L. Scott (Austin, Texas, and London, 1968), 53-54.

4

The reason why it will not do so is simple: the storyteller constantly has his characters puzzled by problems of justice. In the first dervish's tale the vizier's eye-for-an-eye justice is presented as contemptible villainy. It is the storyteller's conviction as well as ours that the vizier acts out of sheer vengefulness, that a just man would have inquired whether the damage was done with malicious intent. The second dervish also gets his share of moral perplexity. The jinni explains that jinn are permitted by their law to kill deceiving wives, but it is not at all clear that they must first chop off the wives' hands and feet; and it is clear that the storyteller's sympathy goes to the guilty lady who bravely refuses to implicate the hero. Even the good demoness in the first lady's tale is limited in her capacity for tempering justice with clemency. She stops short of killing the wicked sisters in order to spare the lady the grief she would feel for them, but threatens the lady with the most dismal punishment should she fail to give the sisters-turned-dogs their daily lashing. The same demoness, appearing before the caliph in the final scene, declares that the lady with the scars was justly punished since she had broken her promise to al-Amīn. Here again we are confused. The lady is portrayed as sweet, meek, and still loyal to her ill-tempered husband, not at all of a kind with the spiteful, malicious women of the misogynistic tales in the *Nights*.

The punished characters are guilty to varying degrees, but the characters who claim to administer justice are either evil or mechanical. The parenthetical story about the man thrown into the pit is again of obvious importance: it praises a person who puts himself past the automatic application of brute *talio*. We are made to feel when we put the book down that justice is a labyrinthine thing, that many causes and effects and many intentions and circumstances must be explored before a satisfactory judgment can be passed, but that short-cuts are not acceptable.

Now the proportion that the parenthetical story completed—namely, that voluntary descent to near-death is to physical blindness as involuntary descent is to spiritual vision—may be a kind of justice: the justice, let us say, of structure. But the storyteller has made sure that we should also think in terms of human justice, and that the whole matter should then become much less neat than the structure would have it: the three men are responsible for their mutilation in very different ways, and, as human justice perceives the matter, the causal connections between descent and blinding tend to be inadequate. (None in the first case, indirect in the second, and extremely remote in the third.) The justice of structure appears an inexorable *lex talionis* that punishes mysteriously, at unpredictable moments. We can see its point but feel no moral satisfaction as we witness its work.

The clash between the two kinds of justice is of course utterly irreconcilable. Our proportion states a law, but it is not a moral law, and the justice of structure is revealed in the tale as amoral. In episode after episode, the storyteller reminds us that the human mind demands a moral order in which the intentions of the accused and the circumstances of his act are taken into account before judgment is passed. The structural judgment flouts this demand. The conflict need not be explicitly stated by the author: it is close enough to the surface to create a profound discomfort.

The discomfort has its peculiar dynamics. The question of human justice makes us have second thoughts about the meaning we can extract from the invariants that dominate the tale—descent and blindness—and the resulting perplexity compels us to take a wary second look at the many other orders that obtain among the events and characters, and finally to wonder at the purpose of this game.

5

If some of the neatnesses in the story have made us ill at ease, the last one simply strikes us as grotesque. Everyone is paired off. Al-Amīn takes back, by the caliph's fiat, the lady he has beaten and thrown out. The first lady marries the first dervish-prince, and her malevolent sisters become the other two dervishes' wives before the brides can say "sorry" or the grooms "thank you." We almost suspect the caliph of sensing the recklessness of all this: he makes a safe choice and marries the lady without a story.

The dervishes have already demonstrated by their curiosity in the ladies' apartments that they learned nothing from their adventures. Had they grasped the meaning of their descents into the liminal areas of half-death, the inscription warning the visitor against inquiry into what does not concern him would have had a profound meaning for them. Thus all the characters are led back into normal life without a transition: there is no repentance for the bad and no wisdom for the blind. The last pairing off does not bode well. Its neatness is an ironic comment on the other orders in the tale.

The storyteller laughs a bit at his incorrigible princes, but the joke is on us, the audience. We have observed more than the characters have, but we are not much the happier for it. Hofmannsthal spoke of the serenity of the *Nights*;[7] this story, though, has no interest in the serenity—or freedom—gained by detached contemplation of the splendid harmonies that grace a morally capricious universe. The storyteller is content if we make out that in the world a music is playing, and if we grasp that it is played upon us but not for us.

[7] In his preface to the Insel Verlag edition of Littmann's translation, *Die Erzählungen aus den tausendundein Nächten* (Wiesbaden, 1953), I, 14.

Relative Chronology of People and Events

(Many of the dates are approximate.)

622 Mohammed's emigration from Mecca to Medina. Beginning of the Islamic era.

633 Muslim conquest of Southern Mesopotamia.

638 Foundation of Kufa as a military camp, later city, in Southern Irak.

639 Conquest of Egypt.

641 Conquest of Persia.

652 Foundation of Basra as a military camp, later city, in Southern Irak.

661-750 The Umayyad dynasty. Syria as the political center.

701 Death of Jamīl.

728 d. Ḥasan al-Baṣrī, ascetic, and putative author of pious letters, sermons, etc.

750 The Abbasid dynasty comes to power. Irak as the political and intellectual center of the empire.

763 Foundation of Baghdad.

790 d. al-Mufaḍḍal, philologist and collector of pre-Islamic verse.

793 d. Sībawayh, author of the first systematic Arabic grammar.

813 d. Abū Nuwās.

835 fl. Qusṭā ibn Lūqā, first translator of Greek texts into Arabic on a large scale.

842 d. the caliph al-Mu'taṣim. Increasing loss of provinces to local dynasts.

846 d. Abū Tammām.

869 d. al-Jāḥiẓ, prose writer, pamphleteer, humanist; a founder of Arabic belles-lettres.

874 d. Abū Yazīd al-Bisṭāmī, perhaps the first exponent among Muslim mystics of *fanā'*, the extinction of individual consciousness in the contemplation of God.

908 d. Ibn al-Mu'tazz. Flourished in Baghdad.

950(ca.) d. Ṣanawbarī. Flourished in Syria.

965 d. al-Mutanabbī. Flourished at the Hamdanid court in Aleppo.

1056 d. Samuel ha-Nagid, in Granada.

1099 Crusaders conquer Jerusalem.

1258 Mongols sack Baghdad.

The *Arabian Nights* has a long history of development. A fragment of a ninth-century papyrus already mentions the names Dīnāzād and Shīrāzād, as well as the title "Book of Tales from a Thousand Nights." The final stages in the book's evolution may be dated in the early sixteenth century.

Bibliography of Works Cited

The Bibliography is alphabetically ordered. Works are listed under the name of the author, but compilations and editions of anonymous works are generally entered by title. A few works, which have been quoted by *sub voce*, or canto and verse, or chapter and verse, are omitted here. (E.g., Dante, Bukhārī, etc.)

List of abbreviations:

BSOAS	*Bulletin of the School of Oriental and African Studies*
IJMES	*International Journal of Middle East Studies*
JQR	*Jewish Quarterly Review*
JRAS	*Journal of the Royal Asiatic Society*
JSS	*Journal of Semitic Studies*
RSO	*Rivista degli Studi Orientali*

(al-) ʻAbbās ibn al-Aḥnaf, *Dīwān*. Beirut, 1965.

Abū Hiffān al-Mihzamī, *Akhbār Abī Nuwās*, ed. ʻAbdassattār Aḥmad Farrāj. Cairo, 1953.

Abū Miḥjan, *Abu Miḥǵan, poetae arabici carmina*, ed. L. Abel. Leiden, 1887.

Abū Nuwās, *Diwan des Abu nowas*, ed. W. Ahlwardt. Greifswald, 1861.

———, *Dīwān*, ed. Maḥmūd Wāṣif. Cairo, 1898.

———, *Dīwān*, ed. Aḥmad ʻAbdalmajīd Ghazzālī. Cairo, 1953.

———, *Dīwān*. Beirut, 1962. Cited as *Dīwān Abī Nuwās*.

Abū Tammām, *Dīwān*, ed., with Tibrīzī's commentary, Muḥammad ʻAbduh ʻAzzām. Cairo, 1951-1957.

Aḥmad ibn Ḥanbal, *Musnad*. Cairo, 1895.

Aggadat shir ha-shirim, ed. S. Schechter. *JQR*, vi (1894), 672-97; vii (1894), 145-63.

Alf layla wa-layla, ed. W. H. Macnaghten. Calcutta, 1839.

Alf layla wa-layla, ed. M. Habicht and M. H. L. Fleischer. Breslau, 1825-1843.

Alf layla wa-layla, German translation by E. Littmann, with an introduction by H. von Hofmannsthal [*Die Erzählungen aus den tausendundein Nächten.*] Wiesbaden, 1953.

Alonso, Dámaso, "Poesía arabigoandaluza y poesía gongorina." *Al-Andalus*, VIII (1943), 129-53.

(al-) Āmidī, Abū l-Qāsim al-Ḥasan ibn Bishr, *al-Muwāzana bayn shi'r Abī Tammām wal-Buḥturī*, ed. Aḥmad Ṣaqr. Cairo, 1961-1965.

Amīn, Aḥmad, *Ḍuḥā l-Islām*. Cairo, 1946.

Arabian Nights, see *Alf layla*.

Arberry, A. J., see *Mu'allaqāt*.

(al-) A'shā, *Dīwān al-A'shā l-kabīr*, ed. M. Muḥammad Ḥusayn. Cairo, 1950.

'Aṭṭār, Farīdaddīn, *Manṭiq aṭ-ṭayr*, ed. Ṣādiq Gowharin. Tehran, 1964.

——, *Ilāhīnāmeh*, ed. H. Ritter. Istanbul, 1940.

Auerbach, E., *Literatursprache und Publikum in der lateinischen Spätantike und im Mittelalter*. Bern, 1958.

Avicenna, *Traités mystiques d'Abou Alî al-Hosain b. Abdallah b. Sînâ*, ed. M. A. F. Mehren. Leiden, 1889.

Badī' az-Zamān, see (al-) Hamadhānī.

(al-) Bāqillānī, see Grunebaum.

Baudelaire, *Oeuvres complètes*, ed. Y.-G. Le Dantec and C. Pichois. Paris, 1961

Beals, R. L., see Parsons.

Benjamin, W., *Illuminations*, selected essays edited by H. Arendt, translated by H. Zohn. New York, 1961.

Bet ha-Midrasch, short *midrashim* edited by A. Jellinek. Jerusalem, 1967.

Blachère, R., *Histoire de la littérature arabe*. Paris, 1952-1966.

Blackmur, R. P., *Form and Value in Modern Poetry*. Garden City, N.Y., 1957.

Bravmann, M., "The Return of the Hero; an Early Arab Motif." *Studia orientalia in honorem C. Brockelmann*, Halle, 1968.

Chaucer, *Complete Works*, ed. W. Skeat. London, New York, Toronto, 1912.

Cheikho, L. and F. Bustānī, *al-Majānī l-ḥadītha*. Beirut, 1961.

Colloque sur la sociologie musulmane. Brussels, 1961.

Corbin, H., *Avicenna and the Visionary Recital*, translated by W. Trask. New York, 1960.

Curtius, E. R., *European Literature and the Latin Middle Ages*, translated by W. Trask. Princeton, 1953.

Czeglédy, K., "Bahrām Čōbīn and the Persian Apocalyptic Literature." *Acta Orientalia Acad. Sci. Hungaricae*, VIII (1958), 21-43.

(ad-) Daylamī, Muḥammad ibn al-Ḥasan, *Bayān madhhab al-bāṭinīya wa-buṭlānih*, ed. R. Strothmann. Istanbul, 1939.

Davis, A. R., "The Double Ninth Festival in Chinese Poetry: a Study of Variations upon a Theme." Pp. 45-64 in *Wen-lin; Studies in the Chinese Humanities*, ed. Chow, Tse-tsung. Madison, Milwaukee, London, 1968.

Dhū r-Rumma, *The Diwan of Ghailān ibn 'Uqbah Known as Dhū 'r-Rummah*, ed. C. H. H. Macartney. Cambridge, 1919.

Ḍiyā' ad-Dīn Ismā'īl ibn Hibatallāh al-Ismā'īlī s-Sulaymānī, *Mizāj at-tasnīm*, ed. R. Strothmann. *Abhandlungen der Akademie der Wissenschaften in Göttingen*, Phil.-hist. Kl., Dritte Folge, Nr. 31. Göttingen, 1944-1955. (In most years the series is called *Abh. der Gesellschaft*, etc.)

Dufrenne, M., *Esthétique et philosophie*. Paris, 1967.

(al-) Farazdaq, *Dīwān*, ed. 'Abdallāh aṣ-Ṣāwī. Cairo, 1936.

Gabrieli, F., "Ǵamīl al-'Udrī, studio critico e raccolta dei frammenti." *RSO*, XVII (1937), 40-71, 133-72.

Gaster, Th., *Thespis*. Garden City, N.Y., 1961.

Gerhardt, M., *The Art of Story-Telling*. Leiden, 1963.

(al-) Ghazālī, *Mishkāt al-anwār*. Cairo, 1964.

Gibb, H. A. R., "Arab Poet and Arabic Philologist." *BSOAS*, XII (1948), 574-78.

Ginza — der Schatz oder das grosse Buch der Mandäer, translated by M. Lidzbarski. Göttingen, 1925.

Ginzberg, L., *The Legends of the Jews*. Philadelphia, 1928.

Goethe, *Gedenkausgabe der Werke, Briefe und Gespräche*. Zurich, 1948-1954.

Goichon, A. M., *Le récit de Ḥayy ibn Yaqẓān*. Paris, 1959.

Goldziher, I., *Muhammedanische Studien*. Halle, 1889-1890.

——, *Die Richtungen der islamischen Koranauslegung*. Leiden, 1952.

The Greek Anthology, with an English translation by W. R. Paton. London and New York, 1916-1926.

Grunebaum, G. E. von, *A Tenth Century Document of Arabic Literary Theory*. Chicago, 1950.

(al-) Hamadhānī, Badī' az-Zamān, *Maqāmāt*, with commentary by M. M. 'Abdalḥamīd. [*Sharḥ maqāmāt Badī' az-Zamān al-Hamadhānī*]. Cairo, 1962.

Ḥamāsa, compiled by Abū Tammām, ed. G. G. Freytag. Bonn, 1828.

Hamori, A., "Notes on Paronomasia in Abū Tammām's Style." *JSS*, XII (1967), 83-90.

——, "Examples of Convention in the Poetry of Abū Nuwās." *Studia Islamica*, XXX (1969), 5-26.

——, "An Allegory from the 'Arabian Nights': the City of Brass." *BSOAS*, XXXIV (1971), 9-19.

Ḥāwī, I., *Fann ash-shi'r al-khamrī wa-taṭawwuruh 'ind al-'arab*. Beirut, 1970.

Heidegger, M., *Unterwegs zur Sprache*. Pfullingen, 1960.

Hinds, M., "Kufan Political Alignments and Their Background in the Mid-Seventh Century A.D." *IJMES*, II (1971), 346-67.

Ḥunayn ibn Isḥāq, *The Book of the Ten Treatises on the Eye Ascribed to Hunain Ibn Is-haq*, ed. and transl. M. Meyerhof. Cairo, 1928.

Hyde, J. D., *A Study of the Poetry of Maymūn ibn Qays al-A'shā*. Princeton University dissertation (unpubl.), 1970.

Ibn 'Abdrabbihi, *Kitāb al-'iqd al-farīd*, ed. Aḥmad Amīn, Aḥmad az-Zayn and Ibrāhīm al-Abyārī. Cairo, 1949-1965.

Ibn ad-Dayba', *Taysīr al-wuṣūl ilā jāmi' al-uṣūl*. Cairo, 1934.

Ibn al-Faqīh al-Hamadhānī, *Kitāb al-buldān*, ed. de Goeje. Leiden, 1885.

Ibn al-Mu'tazz, *Der Diwan des 'Abdallah ibn al-Mu'tazz*, ed. B. Lewin. Istanbul, 1945-1950.

——, *Dīwān*, ed. Muḥyiddīn al-Khayyāṭ. Damascus, 1951.

Ibn 'Arabī, *Tafsīr al-Qur'ān al-karim*. Beirut, 1968.

Ibn Nubāta, *Dīwān khuṭab Ibn Nubāta*, ed. Ṭāhir al-Jazā'irī. Beirut, 1894.

Ibn Qutayba, *Kitāb ash-shi'r wash-shu'arā*. Beirut, 1964.

Ibn Sīnā, see Avicenna.

(al-) Ibshīhī, Muḥammad ibn Aḥmad, *al-Mustaṭraf*. Būlāq, 1869.

Ikhwān aṣ-Ṣafā', *Rasā'il*. Beirut, 1957.

(al-) Iṣbahānī, Abū l-Faraj, *Kitāb al-aghānī*. Būlāq, 1868.

(al-) Iṣbahānī, Abū Nu'aym, *Ḥilyat al-awliyā' wa-ṭabaqāt al-aṣfiyā'*. Cairo, 1932-1939.

Jacob, G., *Studien in arabischen Dichtern IV [Altarabische Parallelen zum Alten Testament]*. Berlin, 1897.

Jacobi, R., *Studien zur Poetik der altarabischen Qaṣide*. Wiesbaden, 1971.

(al-) Jāḥiẓ, *Kitāb al-ḥayawān*, ed. 'Abdassalām Muḥammad Hārūn. Cairo, 1966.

Jakobson, R. and M. Halle, *Fundamentals of Language.* 's-Gravenhage, 1956.

Jamīl, *Dīwān*, ed. Ḥusayn Naṣṣār. Cairo, 1967.

(al-) Jurjānī, 'Abdalqāhir, *Asrār al-balāgha*, ed. H. Ritter. Istanbul, 1954.

(al-) Jurjānī, Abū l-Ḥasan, *al-Wasāṭa bayn al-Mutanabbī wa-khuṣūmih.* Ṣaydā, 1912.

Kalidasa, *The Cloud Messenger*, translated by F. Edgerton and E. Edgerton. Ann Arbor, 1964.

Ker, W. P., *Essays on Medieval Literature.* London, 1905.

(al-) Khansā', *Dīwān*, with commentary by L. Cheikho. [*Anīs al-julasā' fī sharḥ dīwān al-Khansā'*]. Beirut, 1895.

(al-) Khaṭīb al-Baghdādī, *Ta'rīkh Baghdād.* Beirut, 1966.

Kister, M. J., "The Seven Odes." *RSO*, XLIV (1969), 27-36.

Kratchkovsky, I., "Die Frühgeschichte der Erzählung von Macnūn und Lailā in der arabischen Literatur," German translation by H. Ritter. *Oriens*, VIII (1955), 1-50.

———, "Der Wein in al-Aḫṭal's Gedichten." Pp. 146-64 in *Festschrift G. Jacob*, ed. Th. Menzel. Leipzig, 1932.

(al-) Kumayt, *Die Hāšimijjāt des Kumait*, ed. and transl. J. Horovitz. Leiden, 1904.

Lattimore, R., *The Iliad of Homer* [translation, with an Introduction]. Chicago, 1961.

Lessing, *Gesammelte Werke.* Munich, 1959.

Lévi-Strauss, C., *Mythologiques*, I (*Le cru et le cuit*). Paris, 1964.

Lewis, C. S., *The Allegory of Love.* New York, 1958.

Lord, A., *The Singer of Tales.* Cambridge, Mass., 1960.

Lyall, Ch., "The Pictorial Aspects of Ancient Arabian Poetry." *JRAS*, XLIV (1912), 133-52.

———, "The Relation of the Old Arabian Poetry to the Hebrew Literature of the Old Testament." *JRAS*, XLVI (1914), 253-66.

——, *Translations of Ancient Arabian Poetry*. New York, 1930.

Mach, R., *Der Zaddik in Talmud und Midrasch*. Leiden, 1957.

Majnūn Laylā, Qays ibn Mu'ādh, *Dīwān*, ed. 'Abdassattār Aḥmad Farrāj. Cairo, no date.

A Manichean Psalm-Book, ed. and transl. C. R. C. Alberry. Stuttgart, 1938.

(al-) Marzubānī, *al-Muwashshaḥ*, ed. 'Alī Muḥammad al-Bajāwī. Cairo, 1965.

Massignon, L., *Essai sur les origines du lexique technique de la mystique musulmane*. Paris, 1954.

——, *Opera Minora*, ed. Y. Moubarac. Beirut, 1963.

(al-) Mas'ūdī, *Murūj adh-dhahab*, ed. and transl. C. Barbier de Meynard and A. J.-B. Pavet de Courteille [Les prairies d'or]. Paris, 1861-1877.

Mauss, M., *The Gift*, transl. I. Cunnison. New York, 1967.

Meier, F., "Bakkā'." *Encyclopaedia of Islam*, new edition (Leiden 1954-), article *sub voce*.

Mez, A., *Die Renaissance des Islams*. Heidelberg, 1922.

Monroe, J. T., "Oral Composition in Pre-Islamic Poetry." *Journal of Arabic Literature*, III (1972), 1-53.

Mu'allaqāt, ed., with commentary by Tibrīzī, Ch. Lyall. [*Kitāb sharḥ al-qaṣā'id al-'ashr—A Commentary on Ten Ancient Arabic Poems*]. Calcutta, 1894.

Mu'allaqāt, English transl. by A. J. Arberry. [*The Seven Odes*]. London, 1957.

Mu'allaqāt, with commentary by Zawzanī. [*Sharḥ al-mu'allaqāt as-sab'*]. Cairo, no date.

Mufaḍḍalīyāt, compiled by al-Mufaḍḍal, ed., with commentary by Anbārī, Ch. Lyall. Oxford, 1918-1921.

Musil, A., *The Manners and Customs of the Rwala Bedouins*. New York, 1928.

(al-) Mutanabbī, *Dīwān*, ed., with commentary by Wāḥidī, Fr. Dieterici. Berlin, 1861.

———, *Dīwān*, with commentary by Nāṣīf al-Yāzijī [*al-'Arf aṭ-ṭayyib fī sharḥ dīwān Abī ṭ-Ṭayyib*]. Beirut, 1964.

(an-) Nābigha dh-Dhubyānī, *Dīwān*, ed. H. Derenbourg. Paris, 1869.

Nahj al-balāgha, compiled by ash-Sharīf ar-Raḍī, ed. Muḥammad 'Abduh. Beirut, 1963.

Nallino, C., *La littérature arabe des origines à l'époque de la dynastie Umayyade*, transl. Ch. Pellat. Paris, 1950.

Nicholson, R. A., *Translations of Eastern Poetry and Prose*. Cambridge, 1922.

Nodier, C., *Infernaliana*. Paris, 1966.

Nöldeke, Th., *Delectus veterum carminum arabicorum*. Wiesbaden, 1961.

(an-) Nuwayhī, M., *ash-Shi'r al-jāhilī*. Cairo, no date.

The Oxford Book of Medieval Latin Verse, ed. F. J. E. Raby. Oxford, 1959.

The Oxford Book of Russian Verse, ed. M. Baring and D. P. Costello. Oxford, 1948.

Parsons, E. C., and R. L. Beals, "The Sacred Clowns of the Pueblo and Mayo-Yaqui Indians." *American Anthropologist*, XXXVI (1934).

Pellat, C., *Le milieu Baṣrien et la formation de Ǧāḥiẓ*. Paris, 1953.

The Penguin Book of Greek Verse, ed. and transl. C. A. Trypanis. Harmondsworth, 1971.

Pesiqta rabbati, transl. W. B. Braude. New Haven and London, 1968.

Poètes et romanciers du Moyen Age, ed. A. Pauphilet. Paris, 1952.

Propp, V., *Morphology of the Folktale*, transl. L. Scott. Austin, Tex. and London, 1968.

(al-) Qālī, *Kitāb al-amālī*. Cairo, 1965.
Qudāma ibn Ja'far, *Kitāb naqd ash-shi'r*, ed. S. A. Bonebakker. Leiden, 1956.
Quhistānī, Abū Isḥāq, *Haft bāb*, ed. and transl. W. Ivanow. Bombay, 1959.
Quintilian, *Institutio oratoria*, with English transl. by H. E. Butler. London and New York, 1921-1922.
(al-) Qummī, Abū l-Ḥasan 'Alī ibn Ibrāhīm, *Tafsīr al-Qummī*, ed. Ṭayyib al-Mūsawī l-Jazā'irī. Najaf, 1967.
Rasā'il al-bulaghā', ed. Muḥammad Kurd 'Alī. Cairo, 1946.
(ar-) Rāzī, Fakhr ad-Dīn, *at-Tafsīr al-ḳabīr*. Cairo, 1934-1962?
Reckendorf, H., *Arabische Syntax*. Heidelberg, 1921.
Ritter, H., *Das Meer der Seele*. Leiden, 1955.
——, *Über die Bildersprache Niẓamis*. Berlin-Leipzig, 1927.
Rūmī, Jalāladdīn, *Selected Poems from the Dīvāni Shamsi Tabrīz*, ed. and transl. R. A. Nicholson. Cambridge, 1898.
Russian Formalist Criticism, ed. and transl. L. T. Lemon and M. J. Reis. Lincoln, Nebraska, 1965.
Sa'īd, 'Alī Aḥmad, *Muqaddima lish-shi'r al-'arabī*. Beirut, 1971.
(as-) Sarrāj, Abū Naṣr, *Kitāb al-luma' fī t-taṣawwuf*, ed. R. A. Nicholson. London, 1914.
(aṣ-) Ṣanawbarī, *Dīwān*, ed. Iḥsān 'Abbās. Beirut, 1970.
Saundaryalahari, or Flood of Beauty, ed. and transl. W. N. Brown. Cambridge, Mass., 1958.
Saussure, F. de, *Cours de linquistique générale*, ed. C. Bally and A. Sechehaye. Paris, 1962.
Schlegel, F. von, *Über das Studium der griechischen Poesie*. Godesberg, 1947.
(ash-) Shahrastānī, *Kitāb al-milal wan-niḥal*, ed. W. Cureton. London, 1846.
(ash-) Shanfarā, *Lāmīyat al-'arab*, with commentaries by Zamakhsharī and al-Mubarrad. Istanbul, 1883.

Sh^{e}mu'el ha-Nagid, *Divan (Ben T^{e}hillim)*, ed. D. Yarden. Jerusalem, 1966.

Shi'r al-khawārij, ed. Iḥsān 'Abbās. Beirut, 1963(?).

ha-Shira ha-'ibrit bi-Sfarad u-bi-Provans, ed. H. Shirman. Jerusalem and Tel Aviv, 1961.

Singleton, C. S., "Dante: Within Courtly Love and Beyond." Pp. 43-54 in *The Meaning of Courtly Love*, ed. F. X. Newman. Albany, N.Y., 1968.

(as-) Suhrawardī, Shihāb ad-Dīn Yaḥyā, *Opera metaphysica et mystica*, ed. H. Corbin. Vol. I published in Istanbul, 1945; vol. II in Tehran, 1952.

(as-) Sulami, Muḥammad ibn al-Ḥusayn, *Kitāb ṭabaqāt aṣ-ṣūfīya*, ed. J. Pedersen. Leiden, 1960.

(at-) Tanūkhī, Abū 'Alī l-Muḥassin, *Kitāb jamī' at-tawārikh al-musammā bi-nishwār al-muḥāḍara wa-akhbār al-mudhākara*, ed. D. S. Margoliouth. London, 1921.

(at-) Tawḥīdī, Abū Ḥayyān, *Kitāb al-imtā' wal-mu'ānasa*, ed. Aḥmad Amīn, and Aḥmad az-Zayn. Cairo, 1953.

Testament of Solomon, transl. F. C. Conybeare. *JQR*, XI (1898), 1-45.

(ath-) Tha'ālibī, *Kitāb an-nihāya fī t-ta'rīḍ wal-kināya*. Mecca, 1884.

(ath-) Tha'labī, *Qiṣaṣ al-anbiyā'*. Būlāq, 1869.

(ath-) Thaqafī, Aḥmad ibn Muḥammad al-Jurjānī, *al-Muntakhab min kināyāt al-udabā' wa-ishārāt al-bulaghā'*. Cairo, 1908.

'Umar ibn abī Rabī'a, *Der Diwan des 'Umar ibn abi Rebi'a*, ed. P. Schwarz. Leipzig, 1901-1909.

'Urwa ibn al-Ward, *Dīwān*, ed. 'Abdalmu'īn al-Mallūḥī. Damascus, 1966.

Vadet, J.-C., *L'esprit courtois en Orient dans les cinq premiers siècles de l'Hégire*. Paris, 1968.

Vajda, G., "Les zindiqs en pays d'Islam au debut de la période abbaside." *RSO*, XVII (1937), 173-229.

Wagner, E., *Abū Nuwās*. Wiesbaden, 1965.

The Wakefield Pageants in the Towneley Cycle, ed. A. C. Cawley. Manchester, 1958.

Wellhausen, J., *The Arab Kingdom and Its Fall*, transl. M. Graham Weir. Calcutta, 1927.

Wolfson, H., "The Terms *taṣawwur* and *taṣdīq* in Arabic Philosophy and Their Greek, Latin, and Hebrew Equivalents." *Moslem World*, XXXIII (1943), 114-28.

Wright, W., *A Grammar of the Arabic Language*, 3rd ed. Cambridge, 1964.

Yāqūt, Ibn 'Abdallāh ar-Rūmī, *Mu'jam al-buldān*. Beirut, 1955-1957.

(az-) Zamakhsharī *al-Kashshāf 'an ḥaqā'iq ghawāmiḍ at-tanzīl wa-'uyūn al-aqāwīl fī wujūh at-ta'wīl*. Beirut, 1947.

Index

Princeton Essays in Literature

The Orbit of Thomas Mann. By Erich Kahler

On Four Modern Humanists: Hofmannsthal, Gundolf, Curtius, Kantorowicz. Edited by Arthur R. Evans, Jr.

Flaubert and Joyce: The Rite of Fiction. By Richard Cross

A Stage for Poets: Studies in the Theatre of Hugo and Musset. By Charles Affron

Hofmannsthal's Novel "Andreas." By David Miles

On Gide's "Prométhée": Private Myth and Public Mystification. By Kurt Weinberg

Kazantzakis and the Linguistic Revolution in Greek Literature. By Peter Bien

Modern Greek Writers. Edited by Edmund Keeley and Peter Bien

Wallace Stevens and the Symbolist Imagination. By Michel Benamou

The Inner Theatre of Recent French Poetry. By Mary Ann Caws

Cervantes' Christian Romance: A Study of "Persiles y Sigismunda." By Alban K. Forcione

The Prison-House of Language: A Critical Account of Structuralism and Russian Formalism. By Fredric Jameson

Ezra Pound and the Troubadour Tradition. By Stuart Y. McDougal

The Poetic World of Boris Pasternak. By Olga Raevsky Hughes

Wallace Stevens: Imagination and Faith. By Adalaide Kirby Morris

On the Art of Medieval Arabic Literature. By Andras Hamori

The Aesthetics of György Lukács. By Bela Kiralyfalvi

Achilles' Choice: Examples of Modern Tragedy. By David Lenson

Library of Congress Cataloging in Publication Data

Hamori, Andras, 1940-
On the art of medieval arabic literature

(Princeton essays in literature)
Bibliography: p.
1. Arabic poetry—History and criticism.
2. Arabian nights. I. Title.
PJ7541.H34 892'.7'1309 73-2484
ISBN 0-691-06264-1